Jan van Eyck, Madonna in the Church.
An early work of the artist (born 1390)
interpreting the cathedral, the epitome
of Gothic architecture, not only as the shrine
of the crowned Madonna and divine Child,
but as the scene of supernatural events,
raising it to the status of a heavenly Jerusalem.
This is true to the exalted rôle assigned
by Gothic religious conceptions to
cathedral construction.

BUILDINGS OF EUROPE

GOTHIC EUROPE

With an Introduction by
KURT GERSTENBERG

Edited by
HARALD BUSCH AND BERND LOHSE

With Commentaries on the Illustrations by
HELMUT DOMKE

LONDON
B. T. BATSFORD LTD

TRANSLATED BY P. GORGE

FIRST PUBLISHED, 1959

© UMSCHAU VERLAG · FRANKFURT AM MAIN 1958

PRINTED AND BOUND IN GERMANY
BY BRÖNNERS DRUCKEREI (INH. BREIDENSTEIN) · FRANKFURT AM MAIN
FOR THE PUBLISHERS B. T. BATSFORD LTD
4 FITZHARDINGE STREET, PORTMAN SQUARE, LONDON, W. 1

INTRODUCTION

The Gothic style originated in a small, clearly defined region in North-Eastern France. The attempt to replace the hitherto low-pitched roof of the basilica with a cross vault, to give it dignity and permanence, marks the beginning of one of the most fundamental changes in the history of European art, and, indeed, of very much more than art only. Europe's Gothic churches bear witness of this change.

Everything, in the Gothic, stands in the service of an ideal concept of architecture. An overflowing intensity of faith produced a state of mind that saw in this life but a preparation for the next. This mood produced strength for the sacrifices necessary in the construction of new churches throughout Europe. A feeling that all human action was governed by a higher plan permeated the faith of the Gothic period. Secular art, and even popular art, were therefore under the spell of Church art. The sculptures in the cathedral and on the façade are component parts of the architecture in which carving is merely the servant of the building. The cathedral, in turn, serves to make evident the longing for a new union in God. It is the image of Heaven on Earth.

Although the attempt to achieve unity within the Christian Church through the Crusades failed, it had broadened the outlook of Medieval Man. The hope for unity in another sphere was fulfilled.

The longing for another world pulsates through all medieval art, an art that always wants to transcend the ordinary, to point to Eternity. The cathedral is the great ship full of people – the 'nave' – ready at any moment to sail into the next world.

Art is merely one way of giving expression to the spirit of the age. A style, like everything else, is the product of the philosophy of its time.

Cross rib, pointed arch and flying buttress do not in themselves make up the Gothic style, they are merely structural elements, transformed by Gothic art. Proportions and dimensions, of space no less than of mass, are always of decisive importance in Gothic architecture. Indeed, the general impression is dominated far more by spatial relationships than by the outer walls, although it is only the latter that give the building its individuality.

One of the principal features of the Gothic is the increasing awareness of form: the maturity of a building within a certain period can be gauged from the detail on the clustered piers and the ribs, the curve of the pointed arches and, in the larger cathedrals, the amount, and increasing delicacy, of the tracery. The transformation of the sturdy supports at Chartres into Amiens' arched buttresses, that seem to strive upwards in ceaseless movement, and finally into the breath-taking structures at Cologne illustrates this development very clearly.

The Gothic is a style of continuous movement, of lines that must be experienced in the force of their direction, for the strength of Gothic forms is the strength of the men who created them. All Gothic art is rooted in Man, not only in his physical form, but also in his striving.

All heaviness, all solidity, is alien to the Gothic. Gothic interiors may be deliberately narrow and are yet neither oppressive nor dark. The emphasis is not on walls and ceiling, but on the portions that breathe, on the light-flooded and airy parts. The Gothic builder therefore aims at bringing movement into the stone, at creating tension between the different components rather than at giving form.

Form, too, in Gothic, is achieved in a way uniquely its own. Romanesque forms derive from the solid stone block. There is not much detail, the ornament of the walls and piers of the Romanesque Cathedral is still dormant, is merely indicated. Gothic architecture — in contrast to the Romanesque — is essentially dynamic, is flowing motion. The nave-walls of English and French Cathedrals dissolve almost completely and even the last remaining piece of solid horizontal wall is transformed into the triforium. The intricacy of the West front at twin-towered cathedrals like York, Cologne and Reims is beyond any description. It is as if each storey were formed by thousands of tiny separate worlds, each leading an independent existence. This expresses a basic principle of Gothic art: beauty exists for its own sake, it exists, even though no human eye may see what is, above all, meant for the eye of the Creator.

Gothic art is often called an essentially religious art, an art that is scarcely rooted in this world. Such statements should not be made too rashly. It is questionable whether the 'religious' element as such can be expressed in architecture. Such views, in any case, are often based on literary associations.

Gothic artists observed and enjoyed the world around them. But their work, inevitably, reflects the intense faith of the age.

Undoubtedly, there are links between the architecture and the philosophy of all times. Gothic architecture and Scholasticism breathe the same spirit. The Scholastics, too, were concerned with beauty, the beauty of human thought. One of their greatest philosophers wrote a treatise on beauty *(De Pulchro)*. Men who could thus see beauty both in the physical world and in thought, could also experience the higher beauty that is the essence of everything Gothic.

KURT GERSTENBERG

FORERUNNERS OF THE GOTHIC (ills. 2—5). In art, the beginning of a new epoch cannot be fixed at a certain date. Everything is the product of a long development and it is often difficult to tell when the first step was taken. We know when this happened in the case of the Gothic. The abbey church of Saint Denis, the work of the Abbot Suger (1085—1151), can be considered the first Gothic building. But its structural elements, such as ribs, pointed arch and flying buttresses — here transformed in a typically Gothic manner into a light and airy composition — already appear in the architecture of the most vigorous and imaginative of all Western tribes of the time, the Normans.

The Normans had the most far-reaching influence on Early French architecture. These Scandinavian Vikings — Christian converts and settled in Normandy since 911 — transformed some of their almost primaeval energy into art. The Early Romanesque abbey church of Jumièges, near the Seine estuary, was begun in 1040. The vaulting shafts on the triforium are like an anticipation of the Gothic enlivening and dissolution of the walls, although we must realise that here — as in all early Norman architecture and in the case of a German cathedral, Speyer (1024—56) — it is a question of decorative rather than structural features. The great aims of the Gothic, the transcending of space and mass, meant nothing to Norman cathedral builders. But it is the beginning of the transformation of the solid Romanesque wall into a composition of light and shade. These Norman buildings retained a very Romanesque principle, characteristically preserved in English Gothic. If we look at the towers of Tournai cathedral (ill. 2), a building grown out of the Norman tradition, we shall find that they seem composed of separate stone cubes, although their arcades already anticipate the future. This is characteristic of the still rigidly geometric approach of the age. The components of Gothic churches no longer form separate entities, but flow into each other.

Norman cathedral builders already developed an essentially Gothic trait: twin towers above the West front as at Ste Trinité, Caen (ill. 3), begun in 1050 were to become a characteristic feature of all Gothic churches. At Ste Trinité, the massiveness and severity of the rest of the building remain fully preserved. It is not surprising that English cathedrals show such strong Norman influence. Churches sprung up very quickly after the Norman Conquest. Next to Peterborough, Ely Cathedral is probably the finest example of the mature Norman-Late Romanesque style. The magnificent Western tower (ill. 5), dating from the third quarter of the twelfth century, has been dissolved into a network of arcades. It breathes the same spirit as the towers of Laon. In England, such preparation for the Gothic extended even to technical details. Ribbed vaulting, considered by enthusiastic French nineteenth-century scholars

as the only criterion of 'Gothic', already occurs on the Eastern portion (1104) and the nave (1133) of Durham Cathedral (ill. 4). Here, too, an important reservation must be made: the ribs do not support the vaulting, they do not make it less substantial and more tent-like. They are merely attached to it. But the tendency is already there. A path is being prepared, and it needs only a small step towards the fulfilment of the Gothic, towards full awareness of new structural possibilities and their creative use.

SAINT DENIS AND EARLY GOTHIC (ills. 14, 15, 18, 30, 32, 33). The abbey church of S. Denis — to-day a shabby Paris suburb — is the first example of a new interpretation of space. Although the building inspired enthusiasm even before it was completed, its real significance was not fully grasped for many years. It was commissioned by the Abbot Suger, who has left us a description of the church, which rose within the incredibly short time of ten years (1135—1145). But he forgot to tell us the name of the architect, who boldly pierced the heavy Romanesque

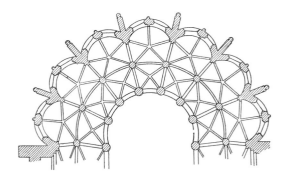

S. D e n i s. Plan showing the vaulting of the Choir Ambulatory, with its chapels. The use of a cruciform rib vault over this area permitted a much greater degree of lighting of the choir than had been possible in Romanesque times.

walls of the choir and thus let the light into a hitherto dark area. The structural advantages of rib and pointed arch seem to have been used almost unconsciously to this end.

Only fragments are left of Suger's building. The cathedral of Sens (ill. 15), which was begun in 1142 and has many features in common with S. Denis, can give us some idea of the light and 'Gothic' quality of its choir. The exterior of the choir of the slightly later cathedral of Noyon (ill. 14) with its radiating chapels, too, shows the influence of S. Denis. Noyon is also important in other respects. It shows the first use of the triforium, an arcaded gallery between the sloping roof over the aisles and the aisle vaulting. Visually, it serves to dissolve the wall. Cathedrals now went up in rapid succession. The walls of most of them are divided into three stories, rising upwards beyond arcades and galleries, thus losing some of their weightiness. Shafts, clustered piers and cross ribs, now used as structural elements, resist the pressure of the vaulting, flying buttresses support the walls.

This period, still restrained in its striving for height, and still concerned with exploiting new discoveries, is called Early Gothic. It culminated in Notre-Dame-de-Paris (ill. 33), the last of the Early Gothic cathedrals. Notre Dame was begun in 1163 under Bishop Maurice de Sully. Its interior, by contrast to Noyen and Sens, reflects the new development already very clearly. The arcades are slender and elegant, the walls of the nave rise boldly and seem almost weightless. Certainly, the West Front (ill. 30) — not begun until 1200 and famed for its well-balanced proportions — still retains some of the discipline of Romanesque build-

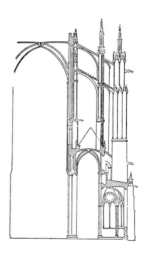

Beauvais. Section through the Choir of the aisled Gothic basilica. The flying buttresses transfer the thrust of the vault, over the aisle, to the buttresses proper.

ings. But the rose window is lighter and more ethereal than any other before or since. The stone has been transformed into delicate filigree. Like many other cathedrals, Notre Dame has no spires, perhaps because enthusiasm had flagged after so many generations of building. Indeed, the thirteenth century in France was an exhausted age, both in politics and in architecture. But it is also probable that the next generations realised that the cathedrals looked far better without spires. The plan at Notre Dame is more disciplined, bolder and more precise than at Noyon and Sens. The façades of the transept (ill. 32) hardly project beyond the nave walls. The transept is almost precisely half-way between the apse and the twin towers. Choir and nave are thus roughly the same length. The tendency is clear: the balanced proportions, the avoidance of an abrupt division between Western, Central and Eastern portion and the dissolution of the wall endow the interior with a movement that is characteristic of mature Gothic art. Apart from the Gothic of the Ile de France, there is another, Burgundian, development, of which Lausanne Cathedral (ill. 18), built 1175—1275, is an example.

LAON AND THE BEGINNINGS OF THE GOTHIC IN GERMANY (ills. 8—11, 19, 98). It is often said of Laon Cathedral (built after 1170), which has influenced contemporary German cathedral builders more than any other structure, that it is still essentially a Romanesque work. But is a purely Gothic building and roughly marks the same stage of development as Notre Dame. Undoubtedly, like the architect of Notre Dame, the master of Laon considered the nave walls at Noyon and Sens still too solid. To make them lighter and to bring the interior to life (ill. 8), he took a dramatic step: although he retained the sexpartite vault and divided the clustered piers with shaft-rings, he dispensed with transverse arches and alternating supports, which had still been used at Noyon. But despite these Gothic elements, Laon remains deeply rooted in the Norman-Romanesque tradition. This becomes clear, when we compare the façade (ill. 9), completed in 1225, with S. Etienne or Ste Trinité at Caen. It is the same structural rhythm. Yet something is happening! Movement has come into the stone cubes of the towers, the corners have suddenly opened. Animals, whose meaning is now lost to us, look down from the pinnacles, the solid form loses its heaviness, everything is brought into a rhythmic order, but with strict adherence to established detail.

Laon, whose style has been the cause of so much discussion, is a striking mixture of Gothic longing and Romanesque forms. It must have been a great inspiration to German cathedral builders. Here they saw Gothic impulses expressed in their own language. Germany, at that time, experienced a last flowering of Romanesque art. Her architects only tried their hands at alien forms most reluctantly, at first in Saxony, where Norman architecture was introduced by Archbishop Albrecht of Magdeburg, who had studied in Paris and under whom Magdeburg Cathedral was begun in 1209. It is significant that the choir at Magdeburg (ill. 19) is by no means an expression of early German Gothic, but rather reflects the struggle between Romanesque solidity and an attempt to loosen it with recesses, columns and openings. The Gothic, as yet, was no more than a source of inspiration. Limburg Cathedral (ill. 11), where the Norman-French spirit of Laon is so much in evidence, and where even its façade comes to life again, still has an essentially Romanesque interior. There is none of the disciplined movement of Laon. Limburg remains a cathedral at the threshold of two epochs. Laon's influence is also manifest elsewhere: the twin towers of Naumburg Cathedral (ill. 10), begun in 1175, were inspired by the French example, no less than those of Bamberg. Germany, for the time being, was wedded to the Romanesque. The tracery in the South transept at Minden Cathedral (ill. 98) recalls Romanesque wheel windows, although it dates from as late as 1256.

THE CATHEDRAL (ills. 1, 6, 7, 20—27, 30, 36—39, 41 to 51, 54, 56, 59, 115, 160, 193). The French cathedral is the quintessence of Gothic architecture. To its contemporaries, it was the image of the Heavenly Jerusalem, created by their own hands.

To realise the significance of such a building, we must imagine the religious life of the twelfth and thirteenth centuries, as it is mirrored in the cathedral. Already the door, through which the worshippers enter, becomes the Porta Coeli, the Gate of Heaven. It is surrounded with large groups of figures, groups that are hardly alike on two churches. A legion of Apostles, Saints, Angels, Church Fathers — indeed, in the words of one of the Fathers of the Church, St. Gregory, even the Saviour Himself and the Virgin — guard the sacred zone between this world, so often only a scene of toil and sorrow, and the peace and splendour of another world, made manifest within. This partly explains the great importance of the sculptured portal. The whole West Front is transformed into the Gate of Heaven. It is no longer an array of the demons of paganism, as during the Romanesque. It serves to teach the Christian, to remind him of the commandments of his faith. Whatever the origin of the separate components of the Gothic façade, whether Burgundian, Norman or Western French — they merge on every cathedral into a very similar picture. Above the wide-opened figured portal with its sculptured tympanum is the region of the rose window, whose significance has been discussed elsewhere. The area beyond, flanked by the twin towers, is covered with statues of the Kings of the Old Testament. A small triangle, indicating the central gable, surmounts it. Higher still, hidden to human eyes, there are figures from the

Dame-de-Paris is the principal character of the book. Rilke glorifies the cathedral in his Duinese Elegies. Elie Faure sings its praise as 'the hero' of France, the ideal image of France herself. Painters interpret it even more profoundly. Jan van Eyck places his virgin (frontispiece), Rogier van der Weyden his Calvary, in the centre of the Gothic church. This surely means that the cathedral is the place of a Holy Offering and that through it Christ's Presence becomes real. Such interpretation has a historical origin. Since the twelfth century, the Host in the Mass has been raised visibly before the congregation. The zealous and avenging God of the Romanesque has been replaced by a more merciful concept. At Amiens, Christ has become the 'Beau Dieu', the Son of God who rules in mildness, surrounded by an aura of peace. The metaphysics of light now begin to play an important part. We only have to recall the third canto of Dante's *Divine Comedy*, the 'Paradiso', or the works of the German mystics.

All these elements united in the interior of the cathedral. The movement that pulsates through its walls extends towards the altar as well as upwards. The nave — in contrast to the Romanesque — is no longer divided by alternating piers and columns or into separate bays. It flows uninterrupted towards the Holy of Holies. At the same time, the wall loses its weightiness, in the 'Classic' cathedrals of Chartres, Amiens and Reims with even greater consequence than in Early Gothic churches like Notre-Dame-de-Paris. The cross-ribs, meeting at the ridge of the vaulting, seem to rise into infinity. The whole church is transformed into

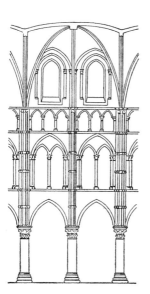 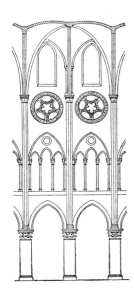 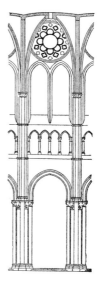

Bay Formation from Early to Late Gothic times. L e f t : L a o n. The vaulting arch encloses two bays. Pilasters spring from the top of the pier caps. M i d d l e : P a r i s. In the bay formation of the intermediate period the plan of the openings continues to be quadripartite; a rose window is above each triforium arch. R i g h t : C h a r t r e s. The bay is tripartite in the earliest form: arcade, triforium, clerestory. The double window shows an early form of Gothic tracery. Each bay has its own narrow arch. The pier and pilaster continue uninterruptedly to the base of the vault.

New Testament and from legend, or heavenly beings. They proclaim that the Cathedral is built not only for the delight of Man, but to the Glory of God, regardless of any human beholder.

Artists and poets have tried to bring the radiant mystery of the cathedral close to us. In Victor Hugo's story, Notre-

a canopy, merely supported by a few piers, which already the Abbot Suger compared to the Apostles carrying the Church. The piers, in turn, are later covered with numerous shafts and thus grow into clustered piers, whence spring forth the arch-ribs and groin-ribs. Everything grows and presses upwards. But no ordinary daylight shines into the choir now pierced, lit-up and finally transformed into a structure of glass, and through the clerestory windows. Here the wall is formed by other matter. It is the splendour of another world that enters the cathedral through the stained glass. All the arts thus unite in the building to the greater Glory of God. The cathedral becomes the 'Summa', the all-embracing whole in the sense of Thomas Aquinas and the Scholastics. Everything within and without had its meaning. The entire world-order, from evil to the most exalted good, is portrayed, calling for the imitation of the 'summum bonum'. This 'total good' of Thomas Aquinas is also the 'summum pulchrum', the sum total of beauty. Although the Abbot Suger's church of S. Denis marks the beginning of French cathedral building, the age of the classic cathedrals only started with CHARTRES, rebuilt after the fire of 1194. Little beyond the West Front with its towers and the West Portal (ills. 6, 7), noted for its statues, remains of the earlier church. Except for the façades of the transept, the new cathedral was finished in 1220. Chartres is the first of the classic cathedrals to dispense with a gallery — still customary from S. Denis to Notre-Dame-de-Paris — in favour of tall aisles and tall nave windows. The interruption of the wall-surface by arcades and windows and the substitution of the gallery by the triforium were to become characteristic features (ill. 27). But harmonious proportions, like those of the façade of Notre-Dame-de-Paris (ill. 30) — another work of the classic epoch — mattered scarcely less. Well-lit, despite the coloured windows, the interior of Chartres exudes clarity and vigour. There is nothing exaggerated, nothing decadent about it (ills. 24/25). The South Front (ill. 21) with its slender shafts like 'the stringing of a harp', was built comparatively late, as was the porch of the South portal (ill. 26), like the considerably earlier North portal (ill. 45) famed for its sculpture. But the most outstanding feature of Chartres is the stained glass, better preserved here than anywhere else. It is not only Biblical scenes through which the light shines, seemingly from another world. A wealth of detail makes these glass paintings a mine of information about the life and manners of the people.

Next to Chartres, the cathedrals of Amiens and Reims are called classic, because they represent the mature phase of the Gothic. They, too, had a far-reaching influence on the architecture of the West. Already the abbey of Upsala in Sweden (ill. 115) had been the work of masters who were active at Notre Dame. A series of Western churches now followed, all based on French examples: from León in Spain to Cologne, and even mid-fourteenth-century Prague, where Matthias of Arras and Peter Parler created St. Vitus Cathedral (ill. 160) — built between 1344 and 1385 —, although the French theme is somewhat varied in the last case. AMIENS Cathedral, in particular, influenced contemporary architecture. It has been called the 'Parthenon of the Gothic', for it reflects the state of European art at the zenith of the Middle Ages, just as the Greek building expressed the spirit of Athens. Certainly, the Byzantine

and the Romanesque church were also meant to be 'Heavenly Cities', radiant with gold mosaic and wall paintings. This longing takes a different form in the Gothic cathedral of Amiens. Even more than at Chartres, the walls dissolve into a scaffolding of slender piers, between which the masonry seems to float upwards (ills. 1, 51). Even the buttresses, destined to lead a background existence as supports of the vaults on the outer walls, are transformed and delicately wrought. We need only look at the different stages of development between Chartres and Amiens (ills. 22, 23). Everywhere, gravity esems overcome. The foundation stone for Amiens was laid in 1220, the nave was completed sixteen years later, as was the façade up to the cornice above the central rose window (ill. 50). Most of the sculptures (ill. 48) were probably finished between 1220 and 1230—1236. They are important as an unusually complete cycle rather than as individual works of art.

REIMS, the third of the classic cathedrals, was at one time the coronation church of the Kings of France, and this undoubtedly accounts for the truly overwhelming mass of sculpture (ills. 37, 41, 44, 56). Reims is also of specific importance to the art historian for another reason. Here, perhaps, the interior shows the most perfect harmony (ill. 39). Here, too, window tracery proper appears for the first time. The present building was begun by Jean d'Orbais in 1210. The choir (ill. 43), transept and two bays of the nave were finished in 1241. The façade, with its incredible portals that seem to draw in the faithful like whirlpools, was also begun at that time. Between 1255 and 1290, the building grew up to the region beyond the rose window (ills. 36, 42). After a century of toil, it was completed in outline in 1311. The wealth of sculpture, the clear disposition of all the components, combined with the flowing

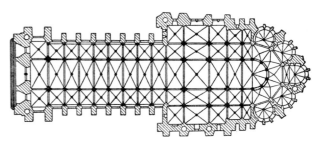

R e i m s. Ground plan. The classic form of the Gothic cathedral, with triple nave, ambulatory and chevet chapels.

upward movement that belongs exclusively to the High Gothic, still enthral us more than anything else. (1 : 1.4 at Sens, 1 : 2.6 at Chartres, 1 : 3 at Amiens.) At Reims, the nave rose to an absolute height of 127 feet, 40 feet more than at Noyon. The tendency to go to extremes is very characteristic of French High Gothic, the classic period of Gothic art. On French soil, this is most evident in the 157 ft. high choir of the Cathedral of S. Pierre (ill. 54) at Beauvais, the most ambitious undertaking of medieval cathedral builders. Begun in 1247, it was completed — including the surviving choir with its double aisles and seven radiating chapels — in 1272. We may well feel that Gothic builders had allowed their enthusiasm to outrun their technical knowledge. The vaulting collapsed in 1248. But rebuilding, with twice the number of piers and flying buttresses, began soon afterwards. Work was abandoned in 1347. It was resumed on the South transept — whose façade shows the characteristic Late Gothic traits (ill. 193) — and finished in 1548. The tower above the crossing finally collapsed in 1573. The nave was never built. The greatest project of the Gothic remained a fragment. The cathedrals of Beauvais and Le Mans — and even the Ste Chapelle in Paris — are listed amongst the classic cathedrals, because they all profoundly affected cathedral architecture. The cathedral of S. Julien at LE MANS, begun 1217 and completed 1270, is not merely a masterpiece of High Gothic architecture. With its double aisles and its vast choir with double ambulatory (ills. 46, 47), it is a true expression of French feeling which equates lucidity with beauty. Dematerialisation of the walls is carried furthest in the Sainte Chapelle (ill. 59), the chapel of the French Kings in Paris (1243—1248). Except for the base, the walls merely serve as a light scaffolding. Coloured glass has almost completely replaced solid masonry.

EARLY ENGLISH (ills. 16, 17, 76, 79, 170). English Gothic developed along its own lines and is not merely a branch of French Gothic, like the Continental schools. This entirely original development of English architecture — hitherto indebted to the Norman tradition — was to culminate in Salisbury Cathedral. It is scarcely affected by contact with Early French Gothic masters, such as William of Sens, under whose directions Canterbury Cathedral (ill. 16) was begun in 1175. Canterbury, despite a certain weightiness of the nave, is the first purely Gothic cathedral on British soil.

A glimpse into the interior (ill. 17) reveals that the clear logic of the French cathedrals has been replaced by a decorative element. The mighty tower above the crossing (ill. 16) is a Romanesque inheritance, always retained in England, sometimes in Germany, never in France. It was not begun until the fourteenth century. The Early English — i. e. dating from between 1175 and 1250 — façade of Peterborough Cathedral (ill. 170), too, is a highly individualistic work. The building's Norman origin may account for its squatness. But it is quite unlike a typically English façade of the period round 1200. The tall, narrow portals are purely decorative, the narrowest in the middle — to which a Late Gothic porch was added — seems almost a deliberate rejection of everything French. One of the finest examples of Early English (described in the caption as 'Decorated') is the nave of Lincoln Cathedral (ills. 76, 79).

MONT SAINT MICHEL (ills. 62—64). The abbey of Saint Michel (ill. 62) on the island amongst the sand dunes of Normandy could be called a mountain fortress (ill. 63)

no less than a House of God. The abbey church with the great Norman tower above the crossing is of some importance in the history of art. Like Jumièges, it is amongst the first examples of the use of vaulting shafts (eleventh century) — i. e. shafts placed in front of a pier to emphasise the upward direction of the walls of the nave — by the Normans. The group of buildings to the North of the church, called 'La Merveille', the miracle, dates from the thirteenth century. They include the cloisters (ill. 64), completed in 1228, with a double row of intricately worked columns, amongst which those at the corners are famous for their foliated capitals.

CISTERCIAN GOTHIC (ill. 128). The Gothic of the Ile de France began with S. Denis. Quite independently, another movement developed. The sober Gothic of Burgundy had taken over the pointed arch from Antiquity and evolved it further. It profoundly affected the buildings of the Cistercian order, which had spread considerably since its beginnings at Cîteaux, in Northern Burgundy, in 1098. By 1200, the order owned over five hundred monasteries throughout Europe. The ascetic Cistercian rule forbade towers and most forms of decoration; the apse was at first square, with adjoining rectangular chapels, as shown in the first choir (1150) of the Cistercian church at Pontigny. But Pontigny adopted the Gothic round choir with an ambulatory as early as 1185, following the example of Clairvaux. The strict centralism of the order caused this type of church to be widely accepted. But Cistercian severity gradually slackened and Cistercian buildings, too, came under the influence of cathedral Gothic. One of the finest examples of this development is the abbey church of Altenberg in the Rhineland (1255—1276), with the lively tracery of its enormous stained glass window and the solemn interior with triforium galleries and smooth piers.

GOTHIC SCULPTURE. EARLY AND HIGH GOTHIC (ills. 7, 12, 13, 26, 28 above and below, 29, 35, 37, 40, 41, 44, 45, 48, 56, 57, 104, 105, 107, 110—114, 116, 180). Saint Denis, whose statues were destroyed during the French Revolution, also marked the beginning of a new approach to sculpture. The new form of the three West portals, of which the still Romanesque portals of S. Sernin at Toulouse, S. Pierre, Moissac or Ste Madeleine at Vézelay seem like an anticipation, was finally decided at S. Denis. The portals come closer together, the middle one gains in size and importance. It is now the task of sculpture to enliven further an architecture, that tries to emphasize the door through jamb, tympanum and receding walls. This is an important aspect. Sculpture was to remain closely wedded to the façade in French architecture. It was again Chartres, whose statues on the centre or Royal portal on the West front mark the first step of this development. A new picture of the world had asserted itself. Gone are the demons and monsters, who had formerly covered jambs, capitals, the bases of pillars, walls and reliefs. Since Bernard de Clairvaux had first raised his voice against the representation of demons round 1140, the conflict with evil spirits took place invisibly within the human heart. At the same time, Man gained a new relationship to Nature and his fellow-creatures. Demon and chimaera withdraw from the gates of the church; at the most, they lead a subordinate existence (ill. 35), to finish as misericords, bench ends or gargoyles (ill. 110). But the jambs now carry patrons of the Church, sometimes even the figure of Christ Himself, who has been deliberately placed in the path of the worshippers. Walls and archivolts are decorated with figures of Prophets and Saints, all closely linked to the architecture of the building. The transformation — and indeed glorification — of the human form into a support of the cathedral begins. Certainly, the figures (1145–1155) on the façade of Chartres (ill. 7) are no more Gothic than they are supports; they are merely placed in front of pillars. Yet they have the quality of pillars, their expression is not that of ordinary human beings. Their heads are those of real people, but of people, nevertheless, who have poise and detachment. It is an interesting process and could justly be called a retrogressive step; compared with the earlier and contemporary development in Provence, the sculpture on the West front of Chartres does not represent a liberation; it does not point the way to independence, to natural forms. Yet this integration of the human form with architecture makes Chartres the beginning of Gothic sculpture.

The Gothic statue, like the Greek caryatid, is the child of the pillar. But it is a reverse process. It has a more profound, more spiritual quality, which it retains, even when the situation changes somewhat half a century later. By then, the figures seemed already permeated with movement, like John the Baptist on the West front at Chartres (ill. 45), a work of the first decade of the thirteenth century. The hieratic stiffness has gone. The Golden Age of medieval sculpture is near, it is coming in the wake of an incomparable creative enthusiasm. Chartres is studded with over a thousand figures. This truly exuberant imagination explains why Chartres had such influence on the sculpture of the West. The stone carvers of Amiens — how close the Apostles of the West front (ill. 48) are to those of Chartres (ill. 26)! — worked there, as did those of Reims Cathedral, whose statues were to represent the peak of Gothic sculpture on French soil. 'Le Sourire de Reims', the Angel of the Annunciation (ill. 56) from Reims Cathedral, is even better known than the 'Beau Dieu' of Amiens. It dates from between 1250 and 1260. But there is far more variety at Reims than at Amiens. Worlds divide the Master af the Reims 'Visitation' with the restrained, almost Greek, Madonna, from the 'Joseph Master', who modelled the graceful, almost sleek, head of Joseph (ill. 44), a work which already goes beyond the limits of the 'Classic' sculpture of the thirteenth century. The group of the Visitation demonstrates with the utmost clarity that the Christian Middle Ages found full realisation in sculpture. A longing for the hereafter has been aptly expressed in the language of this world.

All European sculpture was influenced by this development. It affected Germany, where sculptors had gone their own way and had produced many outstanding works, although there were no schools, and although there was not as generally high a standard as in France. In German sculpture, the emphasis was to remain different. For the time being, Romanesque features were retained, even in the figures at Naumburg Cathedral. In contrast to French sculpture, intended for the façade, German statues were chiefly used in the interior. In Germany — where architecture experienced a Late Romanesque flowering at that time — groups of the Crucifixion and reliefs on choir screens took the place of French Early Gothic portal figures. 1220 marks the beginning of the first Bamberg workshop and, with it, of a continuous development. 'Hosea and Joshua' on the choir-stalls are sparkling with vigour and realism. The Master who created the Visitation (1232–1237) belonged to the second Bamberg workshop — active in Bamberg two years later — whose members had been trained in France. Although undoubtedly in some ways under the influence of Reims, his figure of the Virgin is entirely Germanic, and closely related in spirit to the heroines of the Nibelung stories (ill. 40). The figure of Elizabeth, too, is dramatically exaggerated. She is also known as Sibyl, because of her truly prophetic expression. German sculpture, too, had reached its peak within a few years. Its chief characteristics — in contrast to French sculpture — are strong expression, an almost visionary quality and the reflection of an inner struggle on the face. We need only compare the gentle gesture of restrained sorrow on the Reims requiem (ill. 37) or the calm and balance of the 'Visitation' on the West Portal at Reims (ill. 41) with the dramatic tension of the figures on the choir screen reliefs and on the Founder's Choir (ills. 12, 13) at Naumburg. The Ecclesia and the Synagogue in Strasbourg Cathedral (ill. 29), works of the period between 1220 and 1230, are strongly influenced by Chartres and Reims, however unmistakably German they may appear. It is the beginning of a new type of monumental sculpture — far more subtle than contemporary works in Saxony and elsewhere in Germany — that combines expression with individuality. The 'Death of Our Lady' on the Strasbourg tympanum (ill. 28, below) breathes the same spirit. A comparison with the portal at Senlis (ill. 28, above) — its artist is considered one of the most important early pioneers of French 'Classic' sculpture, which had its beginnings round 1200 — is most instructive. This doorway — in a sense the triumph of the still very new cult of the Virgin — is often considered the archetype of all Gothic portals. The figures already detach themselves from the pillars, the draperies lose their stiffness, everything is coming to life. Less than half a century later, in the Strasbourg 'Death of Our Lady', this new spirit is fully accepted. Even the robes seem dampened to make the body appear more alive. But the composure of the otherwise so expressive Apostle heads is still more significant. The ideals of court life have even spread to art.

X

Wherever we look, the road always leads back to Chartres, whether the Gothic reaches Reims via Senlis and Amiens, whence it is transformed into German Late Romanesque in Bamberg and Naumburg, comes to Strasbourg straight from Chartres, or finally — choosing a third path and by-passing the 'Classic' phase — reaches Cologne directly from Reims. The figures on the piers of the choir at Cologne Cathedral (ill. 57) are now considered to date from the first decade of the fourteenth century. Their movement, supported by the flow of the robes, makes them the antithesis of that sculpture which interprets the body merely as a rigid mass. What was begun by the 'Joseph Master' at Reims has now found its fulfilment.

German Gothic at Strasbourg had one more great moment, when French cathedral sculpture had already passed through its zenith. The cycle of the Wise and the Foolish Virgins was created between 1280 and 1290. The Classic inheritance is still noticeable in the figure of the first virgin, next to the 'Prince of this World' (ills. 104, 105). But there is less rigidity, the expression is softer and less detached — entirely in harmony with the architecture of the building. The naturalistic foliage to the left of the Tempter, too, must not be overlooked. Something very characteristic of this period becomes manifest here: naturalistic representation of the world around us goes hand in hand with an increasingly less sensual interpretation of the human form. This is even more noticeable in the contemporary figures of the prophets (ill. 107) on the centre portal of the West front at Strasbourg. The bodies appear like mere frames for the draperies. All life is concentrated in the hands and faces of the Prophets, who have been portrayed as visionaries and ascetics, surrounded by a world of demons. Strasbourg thus represents both: the survival of the spirit of Classic weight and balance in monumental sculpture — which still permeates the group on the porch of Freiburg Cathedral (ill. 111), a work of 1310 — and the abandonment of Classic volume. In Germany, where the longing for inner expression always dominated art, this new approach to sculpture is reflected in the realistic forked crucifixes, in intensely moving Lamentations and, not least, in the despair of the Foolish Virgins at Erfurt (ill. 113, c. 1360).

This development should not make us forget the almost timeless quality of French Gothic during the already post-Classic period round 1270. An outstanding example is the Christ portal (ill. 114) at Bourges with the Last Judgement (ill. 112) on the tympanum. What lively observation of nature there is in these naked figures rising from their graves, their faces radiant with wonder! But the monumentality of Chartres has gone. It is an extraordinary transformation in the midst of the High Gothic. This was a time when French art had a profound influence everywhere. The centuries of the German Emperors were over. The influence of French culture grew with France's political importance. A typical example: the South portal of the convent church at Wimpfen im Tal (ill. 116, 1269—79) is an 'opus francigenum' on German soil, a German inter-

pretation of a French figure portal. Realism, as it took form at Bourges, also survives in the tympanum relief on the Singertor of the Stephansdom in Vienna (ill. 180) — a work of the period round 1375 — where the influence of the Prague School of Peter Parler was still a barrier to the trend away from 'Classic' form.

What does it matter, if some of the art of this time has only survived in restorations or faithful nineteenth-century copies? The genius of the Gothic still speaks through them.

DECORATED (ills. 65—74, 77, 78, 80, 81, 122, 171, 173). The Early English style, still occasionally linked to French examples, was succeeded by the Decorated. (Decorated, 1250—1340, corresponds to Continental High Gothic.) It was a time when the interiors of English cathedrals were increasingly dominated by flowing tracery. This development began with Salisbury Cathedral (ills. 66, 68/69). Completed between 1220 and 1260, it is the only Gothic structure in England built to a single plan. Spire and transepts follow the same scheme as Canterbury. Salisbury is the archetype of the English Cathedral. The nave continues beyond the crossing in the shape of long choirs, to accommodate the large number of Canons. Like all English Cathedrals, Salisbury was originally an abbey church. Beyond the choir proper, there was a further choir for

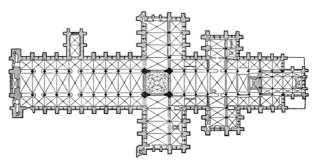

S a l i s b u r y. The typical elongated English ground plan, with its transepts and central tower.

processions and reliquary shrines, the so-called retrochoir. The — usually fairly large — Lady Chapel was placed at the extreme Eastern end, beyond the choir ambulatory, like the chapels dedicated to the cult of the Virgin in French cathedrals. This resulted in long vistas, which were often interrupted by horizontal rood screens (ills. 66, 80, 81, 171), suggesting, rather than revealing, the full extent of the interior. There is hardly any of the upward surge of Continental Gothic. Geometry has replaced movement. In contrast to Continental Cathedrals with their narrow streets around them, the English Cathedral is set in a close, flanked by the houses of the clergy and the buildings of the chapter. At Salisbury, an enlarged version of the French Gallery of Kings covers the entire West Front. The façade of Wells appears like a magnificent shrine, wrought by the hands of a goldsmith. The portals of English cathedrals are usually small and, by comparison with France, insignificant. But proportions and lay-out are very impressive indeed, because of the size of the choir, as the fortress-like cathedral of Lincoln (ill. 77) or York Cathedral (ill. 122) — built over a Norman-Romanesque base in the thirteenth and fourteenth centuries — illustrate. The towers increase rather than diminish the impression of length, since the usual arrangement of rows of blind arcades or statues on the West front — as at Lichfield (ill. 74) and elsewhere — invariably underlines the horizontal aspect. The interior often displays a wealth of noble material and magnificent stone carvings, nowhere more so than in the Angel Choir at Lincoln (ill. 65, 1256—1320). Occasionally, as at Salisbury (ill. 66) and Wells (ills. 80, 81), there are great inverted arches under the tower above the crossing, perhaps a structural *jeu d'esprit* of the architect. Already — it is still the age of the High Gothic — the number of ribs in the vaulting increases, as in the rib and panel vaulting at Exeter. This involves the use of a so-called ridge rib at the point where the courses of the vault panels meet. In England, ridge ribs are generally horizontal. They were already used at Westminster Abbey (ill. 67) and Lincoln Cathedral. Finally, vaults take on the most fantastic forms, as at Ely (ill. 72), where a timber roof was inserted above the crossing after the collapse of the Romanesque tower in 1342. An entirely new system of vaulting was evolved at Bristol, the only English cathedral whose aisles are of the same height as the nave. Each vaulting compartment is further divided into two, the transverse ribs resting on a transom connecting the piers. This, in turn, rests on a pointed arch. The space between pointed arch and transom is filled in with a kind of looped tracery (ill. 78). It might be said that French 'Classic' Gothic draws the gaze upwards, while in English Gothic, the eyes are always led to further and further detail. The lavishly pinnacled tomb of Richard II at Gloucester Cathedral (ill. 173) — a work of the fourteenth century and, like the Constance Sepulchre (ill. 96), a type of 'pure' architecture — illustrates what the Decorated style, with its lively interpretation of geometric forms and an imagination that had not yet run riot, could achieve. It would be surprising, if this branch of the Gothic had not taken root elsewhere. The lower portion of the façade of St. Nidaros Cathedral (ill. 70) at Trondhjem in Norway, although heavily restored in the last century, still shows a link with England which was to be further strengthened in the future, as the fine choir screen (after 1328), a work of the famous Canterbury School, proves. Indeed, English influence continued to grow throughout Scandinavia and the Baltic region.

GERMAN GOTHIC (ills. 94, 96, 97, 117, 127). Germany — no less than England and France — developed her own version of the Gothic. Although the new structural elements were taken up very soon, the buildings retained their solid and static character, when Gothic architecture in neighbouring Western countries had already reached the

'Classic' stage. Even in the first really Gothic buildings in Germany, *e. g.* the Liebfrauenkirche at Treves (ill. 97) and the Elisabethkirche, Marburg — both begun *c.* 1235 — Gothic walls surround interiors that still seem to echo the Romanesque. The Liebfrauenkirche, like the Elisabethkirche modelled on the churches of Champagne, is built on the plan of a Greek Cross, the Marburg sister church on a tri-

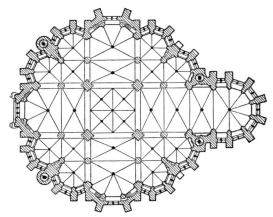

T r e v e s , L i e b f r a u e n k i r c h e. Ground plan of a less common form of Gothic design.

apsial plan — a distinctly conservative feature, characteristic of Late Romanesque Cologne churches. An interesting development took place in the history of the Elisabethkirche; the original plan for a central *i.e.* a cruciform sepulchral church, was abandoned in 1249, and the present nave — with aisles of the same height, a typically German arrangement — was added to the tri-apsial choir (ill. 94). This made the aisles extremely narrow. Close arcading created an effect of depth. Even German artists who were fully conversant with Gothic forms still could not free themselves from the Romanesque interpretation of space. The so-called Constance Holy Sepulchre (ill. 96) is an example of 'pure' architecture, an attempt by the artist to express his concept of the ideal church — a central struc-

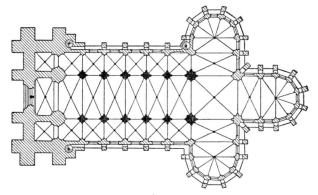

M a r b u r g , E l i s a b e t h k i r c h e. Ground plan (see text).

ture, bearing Gothic features. But the new style was now gaining ground. The church at Haina in Hessen, famous for its well-preserved frescos (ill. 117), was built soon after the Elisabethkirche. The basilica of the Stephansdom at Halberstadt (ill. 123), built between the thirteenth and fifteenth centuries, is typical of the new development in church architecture, not only because of the lay-out, but also because of the renewed use of Romanesque elements. The nave wall again strengthens and solidifies, while the clerestory windows narrow and grow taller. We are in a time of renunciation of the great French examples, a time of the development of national traits. There is interesting evidence for the 'international' character of this national development, for example in France, where the cathedral of S. Tugdual at Tréguier in Britanny (ill. 127), which was begun in 1339, even contains a form of alternating supports.

THE CATHEDRALS OF STRASBOURG AND COLOGNE (ills. 52, 53, 55, 58, 102, 104, 106, 109). Two German cathedrals mark the point of transition from the Classic French style to High Gothic. Strasbourg Cathedral

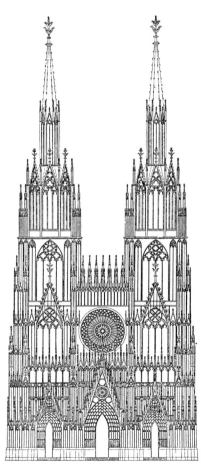

Strasbourg Cathedral. Sketch "B" dated 1275, and signed by Erwin von Steinbach.

— intended to replace an earlier building — was begun at the end of the twelfth century (ill. 109). The choir still has the characteristic Romanesque heaviness. The transept, clearly influenced by Chartres, was added in 1220. The nave — only $2^{1}/_{2}$ times the height of the width of the central aisle — was begun ten years later. Its small height was for a long time considered a typically German Romanesque feature. But a link with the cathedral of Châlons-sur-Marne, begun at the same time, would seem a better explanation. The most famous portion is the West front, whose praise Goethe sang in his essay on German architecture. It was begun in 1276 after the plans of Erwin von Steinbach, and was meant to reach a height of over 400 ft. The characteristic feature of the West front is the architect's use of the motive of the twin-towered façade in connection with the existing buildings, — as the surviving plan (see fig.) shows — to give expression to the medieval longing for height. The Classic balance of verticals and horizontals is completely overcome; at the most, the horizontal lines serve to accentuate the upward pressing verticals even further. The West front — only built to Master Erwin's design up to the rose window — is covered with a double layer of tracery. The power of the vertical lines, enhanced by the delicacy of the pinnacles and gables, permeates the whole building. The entire façade seems turned into a ceaseless upward movement. The solitary North tower was not built until later (ills. 102, 104, 106).

It was different in Cologne, where the choir (ill. 52) is the most outstanding feature of the cathedral. The church, begun in 1248 under Master Gerhard, who came from the Amiens workshop, shares many of the characteristics of

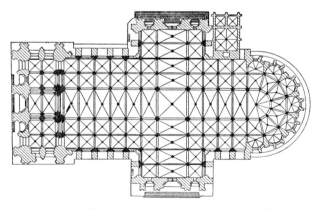

Cologne Cathedral. Ground plan of the late Gothic double-aisled basilica.

the classic French cathedrals. The choir is based on Amiens, the double aisles recall Troyes and Bourges, the windows on the triforium those on the nave wall at S. Denis — but what are comparisons and models in the face of such a mighty building! The nave (ill. 53) has become like an endless narrow gorge. 'Classic' Gothic proportions have been transformed completely. In Cologne, the characteristic Gothic upward movement asserts itself with an almost elemental power. While the nave at Amiens was still supported by circular piers, each surrounded by four smaller attached columns, the clustered piers (ill. 55) at Cologne rise to the ceiling, uninterrupted by capitals or shaft rings. The choir (ill. 58) was consecrated in 1322. Eleven years later, Petrarch said that it was not without justification called the highest known! But here too, a tragic fate was at work; building at Cologne was abandoned during the Late Gothic, with nave and towers only half-finished, and was not resumed until 1842. The cathedral was eventually completed from the old plans. But the new portions lack the vitality of a medieval church, where the touch of the individual stone carver still shows through the general design.

BRICK GOTHIC (ills. 118—121, 157). Gothic brick churches occur mostly in Northern Europe. Their appearance is far more uniform than that of stone churches, whether we look at the severe and dignified façade of the church at Chorin (ill. 118), which still breathes the spirit of monastic asceticism, or the rich brick filigree of the Katharinenkirche in Brandenburg. Northern Germany, Scandinavia and the Baltic, including the lands of the Teutonic Order, are full of examples of this almost dour architecture. One of the most outstanding brick churches is the Marienkirche in Lübeck (ill. 121), begun as a hall church in 1250 and continued as a basilica, in which form it was completed ten years later. As at Soissons — the inspiration may have come through the sea trade via the Netherlands — ambulatory and radiating chapels merge into one hexagonal room. Already the great cathedral at Roskilde, in Denmark (ill. 119), begun 1215 and completed in 1300, was based directly on French models. Roskilde, too, is a brick interpretation of the old motive of the choir, surrounded by an ambulatory. Next to the normally dominant type of the hall church, we find these basilicas throughout North-Eastern Europe. The church of the Virgin in Cracow, with its tall, narrow interior — its triumphal arch is surmounted by a crucifix from the workshop of Veit Stoss, the choir contains the great Madonna Altar by Veit Stoss himself — is characteristic of a type of brick basilica, which developed in Poland as a specific branch of the Gothic, quite apart from the architecture of the Teutonic Order. There is no lack of fine examples throughout the country, from Warsaw to Tarnopol in the South and Vilna in the North. — Brick has been called — not without justification — the material of the German colonisers in the East. But it also celebrated its triumphs in the cities of the Hanseatic league. Not only Lübeck, but Danzig, Stralsund and many other cities raised towering cathedrals. The hard and brittle material explains the lack of decoration and the usually sharply pointed tower. There are few exceptions to this rule, the most important amongst them the Marienkirche at Prenzlau, whose pinnacled and crocketed East front, with its delicate tracery (ill. 157), was begun after 1325.

HALL CHURCHES (ills. 83, 92, 93, 99, 158, 163, 182, 183). The hall church, one of the most important contributions of a specifically German branch of the Late Gothic, already occurred during the Romanesque, chiefly in Westphalia. It also has an early parallel in the cathedral at Poitiers (ill. 93), a foundation of Henry II of England, dating from 1160 and the first Gothic hall church. Is there perhaps some historical link, for Charlemagne had already settled the descendants of Saxon noblemen in the region round Poitiers?

What is a hall church? It is the antithesis of the basilica. Since nave and aisles are of approximately the same height, the nave has no windows of its own and must be lit through the aisles. This causes a decisive transformation. The interior extends in all directions. The eyes are no longer drawn to the altar, which thus loses in significance. But the ritual, in consequence, becomes an experience shared by the entire congregation. The church has become one vast room, instead of a series of corridors and alcoves. The finest example of a Gothic hall church is the Wiesenkirche at Soest (ill. 99, c. 1340). Its plan is nearly square, its piers merge into the ceiling without interruption by capitals or shaft rings. Such architecture does not make an analogy with the mysticism of Master Ekkehard (c. 1300) appear out of place. The first hall churches were small, Romanesque village churches. But a powerful new movement seemed to have come into architecture. The abbey church at Zwettl in Lower Austria is a new form of the hall church, with ambulatory and radiating chapels in the French manner. Its origin can be traced to the Cistercian churches of Walderbach and Heiligenkreuz and the choir of the Stephansdom in Vienna (after 1300). Many South German churches of this type are the work of the Parler family of architects — of the same Parlers who built the choir of the Heiligkreuzkirche in Schwäbisch Gmünd (begun 1351, ills. 158, 163), which is already like an anticipation of the Renaissance. But the finest, most beautiful example of a South German Gothic hall church is undoubtedly the church of St. George at Dinkelsbühl (ill. 182), the work of Nikolaus Eseler and his son. It was built between 1448 and 1492. The hall church had meanwhile asserted itself throughout the Continent, in Bohemia and Saxony — as the Annenkirche at Annaberg (ill. 183), built between 1499 and 1520, proves — no less than in Lorraine and the Meuse region. Its form seemed to have a special appeal to peoples of German ancestry. Linköping Cathedral in Sweden (ill. 92), begun in 1250, with its wide-stretched tent-like vault, is only one of many true Scandinavian hall churches. The 'Irish Acropolis', a name given to the site of the cathedral built on the 200 ft. high rock at Cashel in the thirteenth century and destroyed 1495, may owe its form to these Northern churches. It was undoubtedly a true hall church (ill. 83).

GERMAN LATE GOTHIC (ills. 129—131). In Germany, the Late Gothic brought more ornament. But the true Gothic spirit was weakening. The architect of the choir at Aix-la-Chapelle still tried to dissolve the walls into glass with even greater determination than the builders of the Ste Chapelle in Paris. But the emphasis on line, the upward movement, are no longer the decisive feature of the façades of this period. Instead, we have calculated effects, produced by the play of light and shadows. This is illustrated by the wealth of ornament on the façade of the mid-fourteenth century St. Lorenzkirche in Nuremberg (ill. 130), no less than by the opulent, but noble, tracery of the windows on the South front of the otherwise High Gothic Katharinenkirche at Oppenheim am Rhein (1320–1340, ill. 131) and the façade of the Marienkirche at Prenzlau.

GOTHIC IN THE NETHERLANDS (ills. 168, 169). Apart from the elaborate so-called 'Scheldt Gothic' (i. e. Gothic of the Scheldt region) of Ypres, Ghent and Bruges, which had its origins round Tournai, another, Cistercian-influenced, type of brick architecture developed at the end of the thirteenth century. This is called 'Coastal Gothic' in Holland. The chief characteristics of the rare surviving examples are the wooden barrel vaulting, reaching almost up to the ridge line, and the austere tower. A further development, culminating in the middle of the fourteenth century in the choir and ambulatory of the church at Brouwershaven (ill. 168), on the Dutch island of Schouwen-Duiveland, was the ecclesiastic architecture of Western Holland. The nave at Brouwershaven, with columns in natural stone forming a delightful contrast against the light red brick, was built a hundred years later. It is strongly reminiscent of the Gothic of Brabant. The Oude Kerk at Amsterdam (ill. 169) is based on French models. Consecrated in 1306, it is the earliest example of a 'Dutch Gothic' basilica. Here, too, there is a wooden barrel vault, probably because of the unsafe sub-soil. The light streams through the large windows in choir and clerestory.

THE IBERIAN PENINSULA (ills. 86, 87, 187–191, 198, 199). The Cistercian had brought Burgundian Gothic to Spain at an early stage. The monastery of Santa Maria de la Huerta in the Soria province — founded by Alfonso VII in 1142 — already has many Gothic features. The refectory, with the powerful, widely projecting ribs across its ceiling (ill. 87), is unique in Spain, for its beauty no less than for its size. Although the windows are entirely Gothic, the steps leading to the pulpit are still a typically Romanesque feature, which is also retained in the monasteries of Poblet and Rueda. French Cathedral Gothic appears in Spain soon afterwards. Burgos Cathedral — a building of almost confusing splendour, whose West Front (ill. 188) was later lavishly ornamented and surmounted with spires by Master Hans of Cologne in the middle of the fifteenth century — was begun by Bishop Mauritio in 1221. The octagonal tower above the crossing (ill. 189) dates from 1568, a time when the intensity of Spanish religion was expressed in what could almost be called an architecture of triumph. The New Cathedral of Salamanca was begun in 1513 by Juan Gil de Hontanon and completed

by his son Rodrigo in 1577; the tracery on the vaulting of aisles and choir is based on Dutch examples (ill. 190). At the same time, Oriental and Moorish ornament was freely used, as in the main portal in the so-called plateresque style (ill. 191). Portuguese Gothic went its own way. The enthusiasm for all ornament and decoration, which swept contemporary Europe, reached a peak during the reign of King Manuel I (1495–1521) and found expression in buildings like those of the monastery at Batalha (ills. 198, 199), whose foundation dates from 1397. Cloisters and fountain chapel are perfect examples of the 'Manueline style' where even Indian ornament mingles with Gothic forms. Batalha, in its original form, was clearly part of the abbey of Alcobaça, famed for its unusual hall church with its mighty piers. The choir ambulatory contains the Ines tomb (ill. 86), one of the finest examples of tomb sculpture on the Iberian peninsula. The last great building of Portuguese Gothic — which despite the absorption of features from many lands was essentially a native development — is the magnificent abbey church at Belem (ill. 187). It is the work of a number of architects, amongst them João de Castilho, who was chiefly responsible for its markedly Early Renaissance traits.

ITALIAN GOTHIC (ills. 132–137, 140, 156, 174–177). Italian and Northern Gothic developed quite differently. A dynamic architecture, with its upward movement, was basically alien to the Italian feeling for balance and harmony. It is therefore not surprising that the Gothic only came to Italy gradually. — St. Francis had been preaching asceticism and piety since the turn of the twelfth century. His Franciscan, or Minorite, Order was founded in 1210. Five years later, St. Dominic founded an equally strict order in Southern France. Dominican and Franciscan friars travelled the country on foot, preaching and begging. Their privilege, to appear before the congregation on the pulpit of every church, soon led to conflict with parish priests. The mendicant orders now built their own churches. Like the Cistercians — in contrast to the rest of the Catholic Church — they denied the value of the arts to religion. The Franciscans tolerated painting — where it instructed — but rejected scupture completely; architecture had to conform to the testament of St. Francis, who demanded that church and dwelling should express saintly poverty. Vaulting — except above the High Altar —, bell towers, windows and columns were strictly banished at a council of the Minorite chapter in 1220. The churches of the mendicant orders are long halls, without transepts, but with an extended choir to accommodate the increasing numbers of monks. The severe rules were relaxed in the course of time. But an anti-Gothic element persevered, despite the use of Gothic forms; Italian architecture of the period is a bridge between the related styles of Romanesque and Renaissance rather than a branch of the Gothic. The walls are never dissolved, as the church of S. Francesco at Assisi (ill. 132) — built between 1228 and 1253 in adaptation of Southern French churches — illustrates. Later monastic churches, too, show the inspiration of an earlier Cistercian architecture rather than of the mature Gothic of Central and Western Europe. The open timber roof above the centre aisle of the Franciscan church of Santa Croce (ill. 140), built by Arnolfo di Cambio (begun 1294), appears almost like a deliberate affirmation of asceticism. The chapels behind the choir take the place of the radiating chapels of French Gothic Cathedrals. The Eastern portion of the Florentine Dominican church of Santa Maria Novella (ill. 133, begun after 1278) shows a similar treatment. The spacious interior with its wide arcades recalls the mood of German hall churches. Italian cathedrals are even more 'Romanesque', unless we prefer to call them already forerunners of the Renaissance. Round arcades and transverse arches are an important feature of Siena Cathedral (ill. 135, already under construction in 1225). The shape of the building is entirely determined by the hexagon under the crossing. The lower portion of the façade was designed by Giovanni Pisano. With its wealth of tracery and statues, it is like an antithesis of the similar, but far more severe façade of Orvieto Cathedral (ill. 156, begun 1285). At Orvieto, gables, rose windows and finials are unmistakably borrowed from Northern Gothic, but the geometry of the façade is essentially Italian. Another example of contrasting features is the small church of Santa Maria della Spina (ill. 134). The façade is a veritable armoury of Gothic motives, such as rosettes, statues, openwork gables, canopies and gargoyles. Yet the building itself is quite un-Gothic. Andrea Orcagna's tabernacle (ill. 137, 1359) at Or San Michele in Florence is a further indication that Italian Gothic was moving towards the Renaissance. Very few buildings remain unaffected by this development. Amongst them are the church of S. Petronio in Bologna (ill. 136), which was built between 1388 and 1437 in competition with Florence Cathedral. The influence of the North is clearly noticeable. The somewhat bizarre Gothic character of Milan Cathedral (ill. 175) is largely based on an abundance of decorative features. The church was to surpass all others. Its vast dimensions make it the biggest medieval cathedral next to Seville. The plan, with its double aisles, is similar to that of Cologne, except that the transepts also have aisles. But the lack of light, the gloom round the heavy capitals (ill. 174), the absence of towers and the arrangement of the statues are completely un-Gothic. This pinnacled colossus of white marble with its 6,000 statues was begun in 1387, building operations on the Renaissance façade lingered on from 1550 to 1660 and were eventually concluded under Napoleon at the beginning of the last century. The palaces of the merchant princes of Venice, such as the fifteenth century Ca d'Oro (ill. 176), are scarcely less sumptuous. The most impressive of all Venetian palaces, the Doge's palace on the Piazza San Marco (ill. 177), combines Gothic with Eastern features.

CATALAN CHURCHES (ills. 138, 139, 141). The monastic hall church had great influence on Gothic architecture in Spain, where a definite tradition had already been established by the church buildings of the Cistercians. This type of church with a wide nave, flanked by a series of side chapels let in between the piers rather than by aisles, gained ground throughout Spain, especially in the region round Barcelona. The church of Santa Catalina in Barcelona, begun 1243, is probably the first of a succession of Catalan churches. But the most famous example is the stern, fortress-like cathedral of Palma de Mallorca (ill. 138). Although begun at the outset of the Reconquista, the struggle for the reconquest of Spain from the Moors, it was chiefly built during the reign of Jaime II at the beginning of the fourteenth century. The vault rises high above the basilica plan, supported by fourteen slender, octagonal piers (ill. 139). The cathedral of Albi — 'France's most famous thirteenth century building' — with its fortress-like brick façade (ill. 141) bears impressive witness of Catalan influence in the South of France. Albi has no flying buttresses, elsewhere a characteristic feature of the period.

THE ROSE WINDOW (ills. 31, 32, 42, 49, 106, 192). The Gothic rose window is a development of the Romanesque wheel window, the symbol of the Sun. Sun and Moon, to the right and left of the window, often recall its original meaning. One of the finest rose windows, dating from between 1220 and 1225, the largest and most delicate of its period, and the boldest structure of its kind, is above the West Front at Notre Dame (1220—1225). The tracery, composed of small columns, recalls the new function of the rose window in Gothic architecture. It is a focal point above the main portal, an element of balance between horizontal and vertical tendencies. The rose window at Reims seems light, almost ethereal, amidst the legions of statues on the West front (ill. 42). At Strasbourg (ill. 106), where the rose window belongs to Master Erwin von Steinbach's portion of the cathedral, it has a very special function amidst the sharp pinnacles. It retards the upward movement, it holds the eye back for a short while and thus increases the drama of the façade even further. The rose window above the North transept at Notre Dame (ills. 31, 32), too, is a work of the High Gothic. — In Late Gothic rose windows, we frequently find the characteristic flamboyant tracery, as in the window on the West Front of Amiens, a fifteenth-century replacement (ill. 49). The sixteenth-century rose window on the West Front of Rouen Cathedral (ill. 192), begun in 1201, with its truly magnificent flamboyant tracery, dates from the sixteenth century. It is partly hidden in the illustration by an open-work gable of the period between 1370 and 1420. The rose window kept its function throughout the changing forms of Gothic architecture: it remained the bearer of an ancient symbolism, a point of rest amidst dramatic movement and the highest expression of the Gothic transformation of matter into light.

FOLIAGE (ills. 75, 95, 100, above and below, 103). The stone carver at the beginning of the thirteenth century still used stylised plant forms on his capitals. A hundred years later, a decisive change towards realism had taken place. The triumphal arch above the garlanded roodscreen at Marburg (ill. 95) — unfortunately deprived of its figures — is a supreme example of the resurrection of foliage, which even replaces figure sculpture on the tympanum above the West portal (ill. 103) of the same church. It is mostly vine leaves, that are either sparingly distributed — as at Marburg (ill. 100, below) — or that trail luxuriantly round the capitals of the piers, interspersed with narrative scenes, as at Reims (ill. 100, above). It is as if the stone mason, usually committed to a strict canon, had let himself go for once. — If we speak here of the application rather than the copying of natural forms, it is because nature, in Gothic foliage, is strictly part of ornament. Nothing illustrates this more clearly than the crocketed gable of the Percy tomb (ill. 75) at Beverley Minster.

STAINED GLASS AND WALL PAINTINGS (ills. 60, 61, 101). The glow of the stained glass of cathedrals like Chartres, Bourges, York or Strasbourg suggests a light from another world shining into the darkness. An infinite number of scenes, usually from the New Testament, is displayed in separate compartment (ill. 61). The colours are at first few and strong. A later development brought more delicate differentiation. Drawing in black enamel took the place of the strips of lead — which contribute so greatly to the effect of the window with the Virgin and Child at Marburg (ill. 60) — until all glass painting fell a prey to the illusionistic tendencies of the rising art of panel painting. The art of assembling pieces of glass into transparent pictures degenerated into painting on glass. The forerunners of stained glass are the mosaic and the fresco. The latter lost considerably in importance during the Gothic, when walls were largely replaced by windows. The scenes from the legend of St. Nicholas on the ceiling of St. Maria Lyskirchen in Cologne (ill. 101), painted between 1250 and 1260, have little in common with the monumental paintings of Romanesque ceilings. Here, too, painting is experienced in a Gothic linear manner. It has become the handmaiden of architecture and is entirely determined by drawing.

SOME INTERIORS OF CHAPTER HOUSES AND CASTLES (ills. 84, 85, 87, 88, 89, 90, 91). When the strict rule of some orders was relaxed, the medieval refectory, at first often of a severe grandeur, as at Santa Maria de la Huerta (ill. 87) in Spain, lost some of its austerity. The chapter house at Maulbronn (ill. 88), shows that this even applies to Cistercian interiors. Its ceiling, the earliest example of net-vaulting in Germany, dates from the time of transition to Late Gothic. The refectories of the castles of the Teutonic Order in Eastern Europe — such as the nobly proportioned room of 1320 in the Marienburg (ill. 91) — were probably inspired by English examples. England, at that time, led in the construction of vaults and ceilings. The chapter houses of English Cathedrals are amongst the greatest treasures of English Gothic. The ceilings of these chapter houses — mostly octagonal buildings — are sometimes supported by a slim central pillar, as at Salisbury (ill. 89, 1275—1284), while vaulting unfolds with the characteristic Decorated exuberance, an exuberance that reaches a climax in the chapter house at Wells (1319). The central pier is surrounded by sixteen shafts of black Purbeck marble, whence thirty-two ribs spring towards the ridge ribs of the polygonal ceiling. It seems to the visitor as if he were standing under the branches of a great stone tree (ill. 90). But the Gothic spirit was not confined to the buildings of the Church. The Great Hall of the towering Margrave's castle at Marburg-an-der-Lahn (ill. 85), built c. 1300, is one of the few interiors which have retained a monumental quality that was essentially a feature of the Romanesque and Early Gothic.

GOTHIC CASTLES (ills. 82, 84, 142—145, 147—149, 154, 155). The lay-out of the Gothic castle varied in each case, according to the position. Within the outer wall were the castle wall, an inner wall and, finally, as a last refuge, a tower, developed by the Normans in Northern France as the donjon, a characteristic feature of castle architecture. In England, this became a massive inhabited tower, the keep. One of the finest smaller examples of this kind is Stokesay Castle in Shropshire, built in the second half of the thirteenth century (ill. 148). In Germany, castles either had narrow belfries — inhabited only during emergencies — or were grouped protectively round an inner courtyard, like the twelfth-century castle of Eltz near the Lower Moselle (ill. 149). Regular forms, with cubes, plain surfaces and battlements predominating, were frequently used throughout Italy, Spain, Southern France, in the castles of the Teutonic Order in the East, in England and in the Netherlands, at Conway Castle (ill. 145) in Wales no less than at s'Gravensteen, the famous castle in Ghent (ill. 144), dating from 1180. Occasionally, aesthetic considerations are allowed to enter, as in the case of Castel del Monte (ill. 143) in Apulia, erected by the Emperor Frederick in 1240, the fourteenth-century circular castle at Bellver in Palma de Mallorca with its inner courtyard, surrounded by two rows of arcaded galleries (ill. 142), and the hall of the Margrave's castle at Marburg (c. 1280, ill. 84). But these were exceptions. The palace of the Popes at Avignon, built between 1334 and 1352 (ill. 82) during the exile of the Supreme Pontiff, and the no less impressive castle of the Teutonic Order at Marienwerder (ill. 147) in the Vistula region are little more than fortresses. The desire for decoration and elegant forms only awakened at the end of the Middle Ages, when it found expression in buildings such as the Ünglinger Tor at Stendal (ill. 154), a fine example of brick construction in the so-called 'soft' style of the period shortly after 1400. The roughly contemporary façade of the palace of the master of the Teutonic Order at the Marienburg, South of Danzig (ill. 155, begun after 1280), too, is already an anticipation of the Renaissance.

GOTHIC TOWERS, GOTHIC CITIES (ills. 108, 109, 124—126, 146, 166, 167, 181). The Gothic striving for height finds its expression in the spire, surmounted by the finial. It is like a final emphasis of the dissolution of solid mass. The stone of the upper portions of the spire was pierced more and more during the High Gothic, until there was little left beyond a delicate filigree. French Cathedrals usually have no spires — either because exhaustion had set in or because of later changes in the plans. In the more dynamic architecture of Germany, the spire forms an integral part. The towers of Cologne are like bizarre rocks, thrown upwards with an elemental force. The tower of Ulm Cathedral (ill. 125) — also finished in the last century from old drawings — rises less suddenly, but still gives the impression of a series of rocks. At St. Rombout at Malines (ill. 167), the tower almost seems to mock the laws of gravity and yet has an air of great solidity. This, too, applies to the Late Gothic spire of the Stephansdom in Vienna (ill. 181), the work of a member of the Parler family. There is nothing light and ethereal about the Marien-kirche in Danzig (ill. 166), whose tower seems to rise all the more forcefully as a result. This is characteristic of all Gothic brick churches. But scarcely a Gothic tower can surpass the steeple at Freiburg (ill. 108), built c. 1350, and the model for many other Gothic towers. The view upwards from the crossing recalls a symmetric stone rosette.

The Gothic steeple was not originally intended as a landmark, except in the case of some cities on the sea-shore. Gothic churches on the Continent — but not in England — were built amidst narrow streets. Their portals were a continuation of the street, their towers were meant to draw the eyes upwards from the narrow lanes, as many churches, amongst them Quimper Cathedral in Britanny (ill. 126), still do. To draw the gaze upwards remains their aim, even when the site allows the buildings to spread out and to dominate the sky-line above the profusion of Gothic roofs, as in the case of St. Severi and St. Marien in Erfurt (ill. 124). Gothic cities are always very compact; the roofs huddle together, stacked above each other, surmounted in turn by the walls of fortifications or castles, with the cathedral towers rising above it all. The Gothic Quarter in the old town of Barcelona (ill. 146), formerly the biggest city on the Iberian Peninsula, still gives us some idea of a medieval metropolis. Such scenes show that there was a purpose, in the Gothic striving for height, namely, the longing to grow out of the mass of houses and people towards the light.

TOWN HALLS (ills. 150—153, 178, 179). The tall Gothic towers, the cathedrals that could often hold more than the total number of the inhabitants of the town — they express not only a creative urge, but also a desire for ostentation. The new town halls and guild halls are proof of the longing of the rising Middle Class to give expression to its own importance. In Italy, we find thirteenth-century town halls modelled on ancestral castles, as at Siena, Montepulciano, Perugia, Florence and Volterra (ill. 151). But for their windows and battlements, they might well be taken for Romanesque buildings in their block-like solidity. The town halls of Northern Europe, by contrast, are at times more like adaptations of ecclesiastic buildings. They often have tall roofs and pinnacled, crow-stepped gables, like the magnificent fifteenth-century town hall at Hanover (ill. 152). In the wealthy cities of Flanders, such buildings are often surmounted with a beffroi or belfry. The tower of the Halles at Bruges, — originally a wooden structure, but already rebuilt in stone as the guild hall of the cloth-makers (ill. 150) in the second half of the thirteenth century, is over 280 ft. high. In the Hanseatic towns of Lübeck and Stralsund, we find purely decorative walls without any structural function (ill. 153), pierced by wind-holes and decorated with all kinds of ornament. The Late Gothic town halls of Flanders are noted for their shrine-like decoration no less than for their towers. There is probably nothing to equal the façades of Brussels town hall (ill. 178, completed 1455) and of Mathieu de Laeyens' town hall at Louvain (ill. 179, built 1448—1463)).

PERPENDICULAR (ills. 164, 165, 171, 172). The Decorated phase of English Gothic is followed by the Perpendicular, which lasts roughly from 1370—1485. An outstanding example is the West Front of Winchester Cathedral (ill. 172), built between 1371 and 1460. We now find vertical straight lines in the tracery of windows and walls — rather like upright posts, whose dry geometry has little in common with the Flamboyant style, England's great contribution to the Gothic of the Continent. But the new style displayed considerable grandeur in the nave of Canterbury Cathedral (ill. 171). The nave was begun in 1378 by Henry Yevele in place of the original Romanesque structure and is thus an early example of Perpendicular, a style that was mature from the very start. The large window (ill. 164) is scarcely less impressive. Its outsize dimensions make it characteristic of the new style. Perpendicular was not confined to England, but influenced the architecture of the entire Baltic region — undoubtedly also the mighty fortress-like brick tower of the Marienkirche at Stralsund (ill. 165, after 1382).

THE TRANSITION FROM LATE GOTHIC TO THE RENAISSANCE (ills. 158, 159, 161—163, 183—187, 194—197, 200) is not easy to follow. If we look at Late Gothic vaulting, such as the fan-and-pendant vaulting in Henry VII's Chapel (ill. 195, built 1503—1509) at Westminster Abbey, in Oxford Cathedral (ill. 200) and in St. George's Chapel, Windsor (ill. 194), we arrive at a remarkable discovery: Gothic forms, inspired by upward movement, by the longing to overcome gravity, have been transformed into their opposite. The ceiling, formerly an airy tent-like structure, weighs down again. Space no longer flows freely, but stagnates, becomes static. This tendency is already evident in the palm vaulting of the cloisters at Canterbury (ill. 196) or the fan vaulting in the cloisters at Gloucester (ill. 184, 1351—1377), which was repeated decades later in a more grandiose manner at King's College Chapel, Cambridge (ill. 185, begun 1446). Unquestionably, there is an air of exuberance about these ceilings. But they no longer draw the gaze into the distance, only to detail. Movement has been replaced by decoration. Continental — and especially German — Gothic only seemingly followed a development which, in England, resulted in such basically Renaissance interiors as the Divinity Schools at Oxford (ill. 197). The decline took a different form. The early stellar vaulting in the nave at Maulbronn (ill. 162) is already a weakening, compared to the movement expressed by the cross-rib. The ribs in the vaulting above the choir of the mid-fifteenth-century St. Lorenz-kirche at Nuremberg (ill. 161) and in the Kreuzkirche at Schwäbisch Gmünd (ill. 163) luxuriate all over the ceiling beyond the bays. This is carried even further in the churches at Danzig (ill. 186), Belem (ill. 187) and Anna-berg (ill. 183), which were all built round 1500. The nave has been deprived of all perspective, whether towards the altar or upwards. The renewed emphasis on the solid wall, as on the West front of the Kreuzkirche at Schwäbisch Gmünd (ill. 158, c. 1310), the balanced proportions of the façade of the choir of the St. Lorenzkirche, Nuremberg (ill. 159) — they all confirm that interpretation of space has given way to pattern.

HELMUT DOMKE

GLOSSARY

ALTERNATING SUPPORTS The alternating succession of piers and columns in Romanesque churches; it is a deliberate interruption of the vista towards the altar and was at once discarded in Gothic times.

AMBULATORY A passage at the back of the choir, separated from the latter by columns, piers, etc.

APSE The round or polygonal termination of the sanctuary of a church. It is essentially a Continental feature, English Gothic churches having square terminations.

ARCADE A range of arches, supported on piers or columns.

ARCADED GALLERY A gallery or cloisters, one side of which is formed by arcades.

BARREL VAULT A tunnel-shaped vault.

BASILICA Originally a name applied by the Romans to their public halls. The term was later used for churches. A basilica church — as distinct from the hall church and churches built on the plan of the Church of the Holy Sepulchre, i. e. as central structures — always has a nave, with single or double aisles and a clerestory, and an apse.

BLIND ARCADE A series of arcades placed directly against the wall as a decorative, rather than a structural feature.

BOSS A projecting ornament at the intersection of ribs, often elaborately carved.

BUTTRESS q. v. Flying Buttress.

CANOPY A protective roof above statues, in High Gothic art the symbol of the Heavenly Jerusalem.

CAPITAL The uppermost portion of a column, pier, or pilaster, frequently the subject of all kinds of decoration.

CARYATID The figure of a young girl, transformed into a column or support. First used in Greek art.

CATHEDRAL An episcopal church, derived from "cathedra", a bishop's seat.

CENTRAL TOWER The tower above the crossing, usually more massive than the Western towers.

CHANCEL SCREEN The screen dividing the choir from the nave, usually surmounted by the Chancel Cross.

CHAPEL A place of worship, whose name is derived from a shrine in Paris, where the "cappa", the cowl of St. Martin, was preserved. Within a church, a chapel is usually a small room opening off the choir or the aisles, although the term is also used for separate smaller buildings.

CHEVET A circular or polygonal apse, surrounded by an ambulatory, with chapels leading off it.

CHOIR The portion of the church set apart for the altar and for the clergy. The choir almost invariably faces East.

CLERESTORY, or CLEAR STOREY The portion of the nave wall, which rises above the roofs of the aisles, and is pierced by clerestory windows.

CLOISTERS Covered and arcaded passages round an open space, linking the church with the separate parts of a monastery.

CLUSTERED PIER A pier composed of a number of small columns. Clustered piers are a characteristic feature of Decorated architecture.

COLUMN An upright circular shaft, tapering slightly towards the top, mostly standing on a base and surmounted by a capital.

CORBEL A projecting stone, or piece of timber, supporting a wall, beam, etc.

CROCKET Projecting leaves, branches of foliage, flowers, etc., used to decorate the angles of spires, pinnacles, canopies, etc.

CROSSING The space marked by the intersection of nave and transept.

CROSS-VAULT A vault formed by the inter-section of two barrel vaults at right angles.

CURVILINEAR A late form of Decorated tracery.

DECORATED The Middle phase of English Gothic (c. 1307—1377), whose forms are derived deliberately from decorative motives. It covers roughly the same period as High Gothic on the Continent.

DIAGONAL RIBS The ribs running along the groins of a cross vault. During the Gothic period, diagonal ribs were used to support the thin stone panels of the cross vault and thus were a structural, rather than a decorative feature.

EARLY ENGLISH The earliest phase of English Gothic, prevalent in the thirteenth century; although decorative elements are already markedly developed, the influence of Norman-French Early Gothic is still much in evidence.

FAN VAULTING A fan-like arrangement of the ribs, characteristic of English late Gothic.

FIGURE CYCLE Groups of figures, used on the façade to illustrate a story, such as the Redemption of Man.

FINIAL The upper portion of a pinnacle, bench end, etc., frequently composed of four crockets.

FLAMBOYANT The last phase of French Gothic (fourteenth, fifteenth and part sixteenth cent.), named after its flame-like tracery.

FLYING BUTTRESS An arch starting from a detached pier, abutting against an outer wall. It is a characteristic feature of Gothic churches.

GALLERY OF KINGS A series of statues of the Kings of Israel on the West Front of Gothic cathedrals.

HALL CHURCH A church with nave and aisles of equal height. The type was allready developed in Westphalia and elsewhere during the Romanesque. Though common on the Continent (Elisabethkirche,

Marburg, Stephansdom, Vienna, etc.), it is extremely rare in England, where the only great hall church is Bristol Cathedral.

IMPOST The portion of a column, pier, etc., from which an arch springs.

JAMBS The sides of doors and windows.

LADY CHAPEL A chapel dedicated to the cult of the Virgin, usually — but not always, as at Ely — at the Eastern end of English cathedrals.

LIERNE RIB A short intermediate rib, which is not a ridge rib and does not rise from an impost. Its function is purely decorative. A vaulting compartment covered in lierne ribs is called a lierne vault, or a stellar vault.

LODGE Originally, in the Middle Ages, an association of stone masons, connected with the building of a particular church.

NORMAN Roughly the English equivalent of the Romanesque.

OGEE A moulding made up of a convex and a concave arch. The term is also applied to the Pointed Arch (q. v.)

PERPENDICULAR The last phase of English Gothic (fifteenth and sixteenth centuries) and characterised by its horizontal and vertical tracery.

PIERS A mass of masonry — as distinct from the column — supporting an arch or vault.

PINNACLE A pointed little turret surmounting the parapets, buttresses, gables, etc., of Gothic cathedrals.

PLATERESQUE From 'plateresco', i.e. like the work of the goldsmith (Spanish). A type of Spanish fifteenth-century decoration, composed of various stylistic elements; chiefly used on façades.

POINTED ARCH An arch formed by two intersecting segments of a circle. It is an important — but by no means the only characteristic — feature of Gothic architecture.

PORTAL The main entrance of a church, emphasised by groups of sculpture and other decoration.

RELIEF A type of sculpture in stone, wood, etc., not completely detached from its background.

REFECTORY The dining hall of a monastery, convent, etc.

RENAISSANCE The period following the Gothic. The term — by no means adequate — is derived from only one characteristic of this style, the revival of the forms of Classical Antiquity.

RETROCHOIR The continuation of the choir of English cathedrals, terminating in the Lady Chapel.

RIB A projecting band, running originally along the groin of a vault. In Gothic architecture, the ribs further emphasise the upward movement and thus have both an aesthetic and a structural function. In the Decorative and Perpendicular phases, ribs are often made to fan out in all directions.

RIDGE The uppermost horizontal line of a sloping roof.

RIDGE RIB The rib following the ridge. In English Gothic the ridge is frequently decorated with bosses at the point of intersection with other ribs.

ROMANESQUE The phase before the Gothic, prevalent in Western Europe from the ninth to the twelfth century. The effect is one of solidity and strength.

ROOD LOFT The gallery — reserved for minstrels and singers — above the rood screen or chancel screen.

ROOD SCREEN q. v. CHANCEL SCREEN.

ROSE WINDOW A round window above the West portal or the main portals of the transepts. It was developed from the Roman-esque wheel window, which symbolised Christ as the Sun.

SCHOLASTICISM A medieval theological system which aims at a greater understanding of Christianity through philosophy. The Scholastic movement was at its peak in the thirteenth century.

SCREEN q.v. CHANCEL SCREEN.

SHAFTS (q. v. CLUSTERED PIERS) Originally describing the portion between the base and capital of a column, the term is also applied to half or three-quarter columns attached to Gothic and Romanesque piers and walls. Though at first purely decorative features, shafts were later made to support transverse arches and ribs.

STELLAR VAULTING q.v. FAN VAULTING.

TRANSEPT The portion of a church intersecting the nave at a right angle.

TRANSVERSE ARCHES and ribs link opposite piers or columns and further emphasise the division into bays.

TRIAPSIAL A church having three apses, one for the choir and one for each transept. Many German churches dating from between the eleventh and the thirteenth century are triapsial.

TRIFORIUM An arcaded gallery between the sloping roof over the aisles and the aisle vaulting.

TRIUMPHAL CROSS or ROOD CROSS The crucifix above the rood screen (q.v.).

TWIN TOWERS This feature has its origin in Norman-Romanesque architecture and was taken over by the Gothic. Twin towers are always placed to the right and left of the West front.

TYMPANUM The space within a round or pointed arch above a Gothic portal, usually decorated in relief.

INDEX OF PLACES

Roman numerals denote mention in the text, Arabic numerals illustrations.

This picture giving a "classic Gothic" impression of space makes a suitable introduction to a series dealing with the origin, development, Golden Age and last days of a style of architecture. The upward surge, the transformation of massive stone into the spiritualised forms of cathedral Gothic seem to the onlooker to be the image of divine harmonies. — The interior of Notre-Dame in *Amiens*, the "Parthenon of Gothic".

Foto
Marb

Roubier

Der zum Wesen der Gotik gehörende Höhendrang kündigt sich in der
normannischen Architektur bereits während der romanischen Epoche an,
so in der Kathedrale von *Tournai* in Belgien.

The upward thrust characteristic of Gothic is revealed
in Norman architecture as early as the Romanesque period.
Tournai Cathedral in Belgium.

Das Prinzip der zweitürmigen Westfassade entwickelt sich ebenfalls
schon in der normannischen Architektur. Die Westfront
der 1050 begonnenen Kirche Ste. Trinité in *Caen*.

The principle of the twin-towered West Front
was likewise developed in Norman architecture.
The West Front of the Ste. Trinité Church, *Caen*, begun 1050.

Das Mittelschiff der normannisch-hochromanischen Kathedrale
von *Durham* (1093—1130) in England, bemerkenswert wegen der hier
zuerst verwandten Kreuzrippengewölbe (1133), denen in der Gotik
entscheidende Bedeutung zukommen sollte.

The nave of the High Romanesque cathedral of *Durham* (1093—1130)
with the rib-vaulting (1133) — the earliest in Europe —
that was to play so decisive a role in the history of Gothic.

Eines der reifsten Denkmäler dieses die Gotik vorbereitenden Stil
ist die Kathedrale von *Ely* in England. Von Süden gesehen
Der romanische Teil der Westfassade, überragt von dem gotischen Westturm

Ely Cathedral, one of the most finished examples of this style
heralding the approach of Gothic. Seen from the South
the Romanesque part of the West Façade
surmounted by the Gothic West Spire

←

Das ältere Westportal und die
frühgotische Rose (1135–1155)
der Kathedrale von *Chartres*,
Übergang vom romanischen
zum gotischen Stil.

The older West Portal and
Early Gothic rose-window
(1135–1155) of *Chartres*
Cathedral showing the
transition from Romanesque
to Gothic.

Die spätromanischen Skulpturen
vom Westportal der Kathedrale
in *Chartres*, Vorfahren Christi
darstellend, wirken wie eine
Vorbereitung des gotischen
Figurenstiles.

The Late Romanesque
sculptures representing
ancestors of Christ on the
West Portal of *Chartres*
Cathedral, already bear
indications of Gothic
figure-style.

7   Jeiter

Roubier

Die Kathedrale von *Laon*, bereits gotisch in der Anlage, zeigt in der kraftvollen Plastik des Aufbaus noch deutlich die Herkunft aus romanisch-normannischem Bauempfinden. Oben: Mittelschiffswand und Emporen. Rechts: Westfront (begonnen 1180).

Laon Cathedral, Gothic in plan, clearly shows Romanesque-Norman influences in the massive strength of its stone construction. Above: arcades and triforium. Right: West Front (1180 seqq.).

Seeger →

Hege

Zwei Beispiele für die Auswirkung von Laon, das besonders auf deutsche Baumeister eingewirkt hat. Oben: Das Turmpaar des Domes zu *Naumburg* (1. Hälfte 13. Jh.). Rechts: Dom von *Limburg* (1215—1235). Die Wandgliederung folgt dem Vorbild Laon, die Raumkonzentration atmet noch romanischen Geist.

Two examples showing the influence of Laon on German architects in particular. Above: the twin towers of splendid *Naumburg* Cathedral (first half of 13th ct.). Right: *Limburg* Cathedral. Bay-formation based on that of Laon. The effect of marked spatial concentration is suggestive of the Romanesque.

11

← Hege

Französisch-gotischer Einfluß bewirkte, daß im Dom zu *Naumburg* eine letzte Vollendung romanisch-deutscher Plastik sich entfaltete.
Links: „Petrus und die Magd" vom Lettner. Oben: Chorwand mit den Stifterfiguren (1250–1260).

French Gothic influences contributed to the development of German-Romanesque sculpture, attaining perfection in *Naumburg* Cathedral.
Left: "Peter and the Maid" on the rood-loft. Above: choir, showing figures of the cathedral founders (1250–1260).

13

Der Geist der Abteikirche von St. Denis (Chor 1140–1144), der „Wiege der Gotik", die nicht mehr in ursprünglichem Zustand erhalten ist,
lebt fort in zwei Tochterkirchen. Oben: Kathedrale von *Noyon*, Chor mit Strebewänden. Rechts: Der lichte Chor der Kathedrale von *Sens*.

The abbey church of St. Denis (choir: 1140–1144), the first purely Gothic building (not preserved in its original state),
left its mark on two branch-churches. Above: *Noyon* Cathedral, choir with buttresses. Right: the bright choir of *Sens* Cathedral.

Der erste gotische Bau Englands, die Kathedrale von *Canterbury* (nach 1175), zeigt, neben der Verankerung in normannischer Bautradition, Kersting →
den Einfluß der französischen gotischen Kathedrale. Oben: Ansicht von Südwesten. Rechts: Mittelschiff nach Osten.

The first Gothic construction in England, *Canterbury* Cathedral (post 1175), shows, besides Norman roots, the influence of the French Gothic Cathedral.
Above: the cathedral from the south-west. Right: the nave looking east.

Seege

Gewölbe der Eingangshalle zur frühgotischen Kathedrale von *Lausanne* (begonnen 1175),
die das schönste Bauwerk ihrer Epoche in der Schweiz ist.

Vaulting in the narthex of the Early Gothic cathedral of *Lausanne* (1175 seqq.),
the finest building of the period in Switzerland.

18

Antik-romanisch empfundene Festigung des Gewändes und frühgotisch-französische Grundrißplanung
ringen im 1209 begonnenen Chor des Domes zu *Magdeburg* um die Vorherrschaft.

Classical-Romanesque wall-strengthening and French Early Gothic ground-planning vye
with each other in the choir of *Magdeburg* Cathedral, begun in 1209.

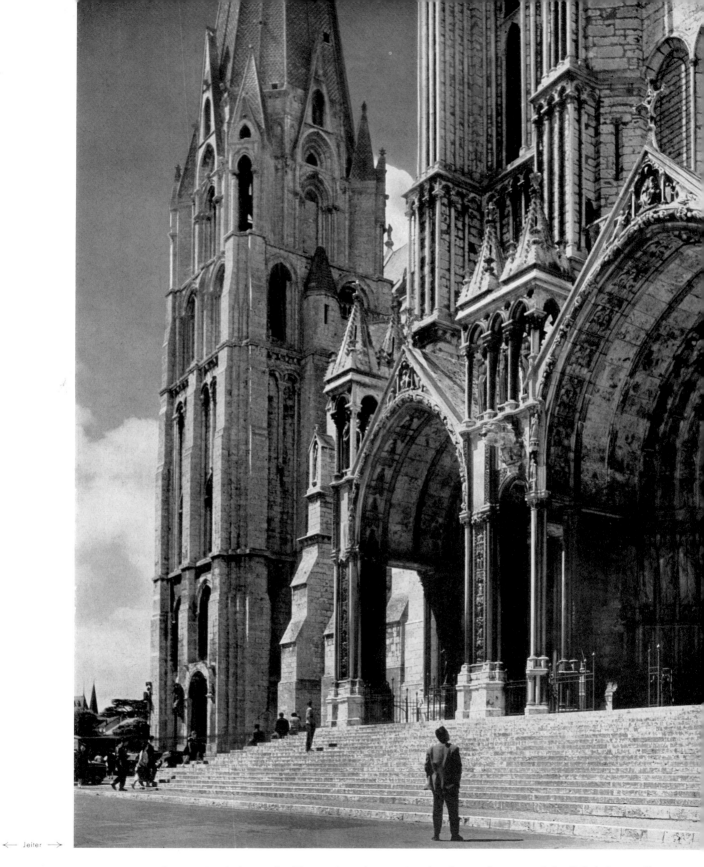

← Jeiter →

Nach einem Brand, der nur das Westportal verschonte, entstand nach 1194 die neue, gotische Kathedrale von *Chartres*,
die genialste in der Reihe der „klassischen" Kathedralen Frankreichs. Links: Südquerhaus von Südwesten.
Oben: Der frühgotische, 1145 erbaute Südwestturm, dazu die Portale des Südquerhauses (1212—1220) mit Vorhalle (1224—1250).

The new Gothic cathedral of *Chartres*, the most brilliant of all the "classic" cathedrals of France,
was begun in 1194 after a fire which destroyed all but the old West Portal. Left: south transept from the south-west.
Above: the Early Gothic south-west tower, built in 1145, showing the portals of the south transept (1212—1220) with porch (1224—1250).

21

Jeiter

Über mächtige Strebebögen wird der Schub der Gewölbe des von hohen Fenstern durchlichteten Chores
auf die Strebepfeiler außerhalb der Wandflächen abgeleitet. *Chartres.*

The thrust of the vaulting in the choir, lit by the high clerestory, is supported
by buttresses and flying buttresses. *Chartres.*

Roubier

Französische Lust am Konstruktiven gestaltet das Strebewerk, das angesichts der Auflösung der Wände nunmehr notwendig wird, zu einem goldschmiedehaften Phantasiegebilde um. *Amiens.*

Buttressing, now made necessary by the immense height of the vast stone vaults, was transformed by the French with their love of the constructive into a fantasy of delicate filigree. *Amiens.*

Der „fließende", organisch
gegliederte Innenraum der
Kathedrale von *Chartres*
offenbart den vollendeten
Gegensatz zur romanischen Art,
in sich geschlossene Bauteile
gegeneinander abzusetzen.
(Zustand während des letzten
Krieges: ohne Originalfenster.)

The "flowing" interior of
Chartres Cathedral presents
the perfect contrast to the
Romanesque type of interior
with its subdivision into a
number of clearly
separated parts.
(Stained glass windows
removed during last war.)

Immer bleibt die französische gotische Skulptur der ursprünglichen Funktion als Säule verhaftet.
Apostel vom Südquerhausportal in *Chartres* (1212–1220).

French Gothic sculpture always has as its original function that of a pillar.
Apostles from the south transept portal in *Chartres* (1212–1220).

Die charakteristisch gotische Wandgliederung
erreicht in *Chartres* ihren klassischen Höhepunkt.

The characteristic Gothic bay-formation
achieves classic perfection in *Chartres* Cathedral.

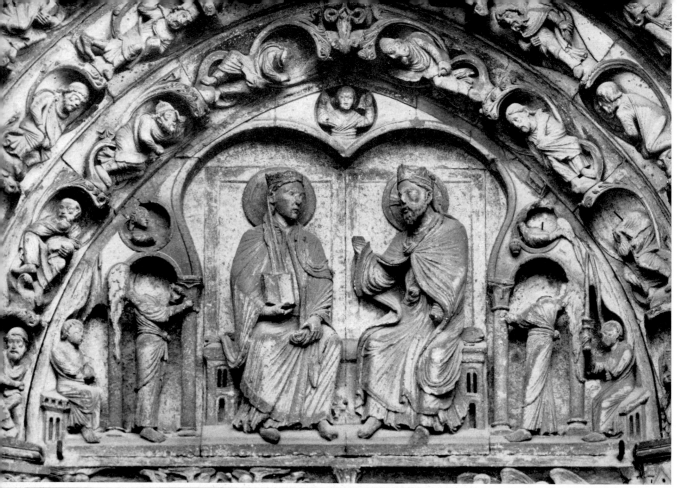

Die Einordnung der Plastik in das Baugefüge
französischer Kathedralen offenbart sich
im Tympanon des Marienportals von *Senlis*
(links oben). Der von einem deutschen Meister
geschaffene Marientod im Tympanon des
Südportals von *Straßburg* (um 1230, links unten)
ebenso wie die Synagoge des gleichen Portals
(rechts) zeigen ein freieres plastisches Empfinden.

The harmony between structure and sculpture
in French cathedrals is revealed in the
tympanum of the St. Mary Portal at *Senlis*
(above, left). A freer sculptural style is to be
found at *Strasbourg* in the tympanum
of the South Portal (c. 1230, below, left),
portraying the death of Our Lady,
and the Synagogue (right), both the work
of a German master.

Foto Marburg

Roubier

←— Jeiter

Als am meisten „französische" unter den gotischen Fassaden gilt die von Notre Dame in *Paris* (links, beg. 1200)
wegen ihres Gleichgewichts vertikaler wie horizontaler Tendenzen. Oben: Blick gegen die Rose des Nordquerhauses.

The façade of Notre Dame, *Paris* (left, 1200 seqq.), is considered to be the most "French" of Gothic Façades on account of the balance
achieved out of two drives of vertical and horizontal tendencies. Above: view of the rose-window over the north transept.

Notre Dame, *Paris*. Oben: Die französischen Kathedralen bilden prachtvolle Fassaden auch an den Querhäusern aus. Nordquerhaus (Mitte 13. Jh.).
Rechts: Als letzte der gotischen Kathedralen weist Notre Dame, wie St. Denis, die normannische Empore auf. Blick vom Chor ins Mittelschiff (nach 1182).

Notre Dame, *Paris*. Above: splendid façades are added to the transepts of French cathedrals too. North transept (mid-13th century).
Right: Notre Dame is the last of the Gothic cathedrals to boast a Norman triforium like St. Denis. View of the nave from the choir (post 1182).

Paris, Notre Dame. Das Madonnenportal (nördl. Westportal)
zeigt die enge Bindung der Plastik an die Architektur.

Paris, Notre Dame. The Madonna Portal (northern West Portal)
shows the interdependence between sculpture and architecture.

Archivolten im Bogenfeld des mittleren Westportals von Notre Dame in *Paris*.
Oben Personifikation der Tugenden, untere Reihe Darstellung der Laster (1225—1230).

Figures from the archivolt of the centre door of the West Portal, Notre Dame, *Paris*.
The upper rows represent virtues personified, the lower, the vices (1225—1230).

Notre Dame, *Reims*. Links: Als Gipfelpunkt langen Reifens präsentiert sich die Fassade (beg. 1241)
mit ihren überaus betonten Portalen voller Harmonie der Bauglieder. Oben: Totenmesse vom Gewände der ehemaligen Kreuzgangspforte.

Notre Dame, *Reims*. Left: the façade (begun in 1241) with its outstanding, harmonious portals is a masterpiece
which took many years to reach fruition. Above: Requiem from the jamb of the former cloister-door.

Die Kathedrale von *Reims* war die Salbungsstätte der französischen Könige; daher der unvergleichliche Reichtum an plastischem Schmuck.
Das mittlere Westportal (1255–1290) zeigt nicht nur außen (Bild oben), sondern auch innerhalb der Kathedrale (Bild rechte Seite)
ein figürliches Programm. Die Stelle des Tympanons nimmt eine zweite Fensterrose ein (siehe auch Umschlagbild).

3

As the French kings were crowned at *Reims* Cathedral, an incomparable wealth and variety of sculptural decoration is to be found there. The central door of the West Portal (1255–1290) is richly carved with figures both inside (picture above) and out (left page). The tympanum is in this case a glass window (cf. frontispiece).

Das Skulpturenportal der französischen Kathedrale dient lehrhafter Darbietung des Glaubensprogramms. Rechte Seite: Gewände vom Westportal in *Reims* mit Heimsuchungsgruppe. — In Deutschland finden sich Skulpturen zunächst im Innenraum. Oben: Elisabeth und Maria, *Bamberg*.

The sculptured portals of French cathedrals served to instruct the faithful. Right: jamb from the West Portal in *Reims* illustrating the Visitation. In Germany carving is to be found at first only in the interior. Above: Elizabeth and Mary, *Bamberg*.

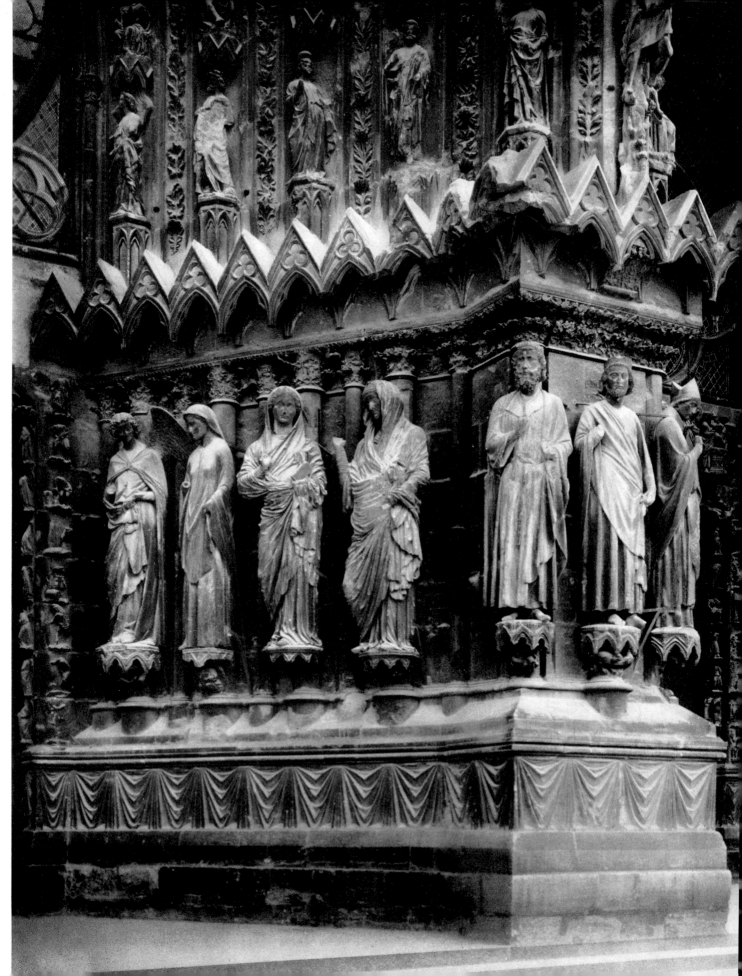

Jeiter

Blick aus dem Chor gegen die 1285 vollendete Fensterrose und die nach dem Vorbild von Chartres „klassisch" dreigeschossige Schiffswand.

View taken from the choir of the rose-window, completed c. 1285, and the "classic" three-tiered bay-formation modelled on that of Chartres.

Blick aus dem Chorumgang mit seinen mächtigen, antikisch erscheinenden Rundpfeilern nach Westen in das Innere der Kathedrale von *Reims*.

The cathedral interior at *Reims* looking westwards, taken from the retro-choir with its massive classical-looking cylindrical piers.

Reichtum und Größe der Plastik von *Reims* lassen sich an Rang nur griechischer Bildhauerei vergleichen. Kopf des Josef (um 1260).

The wealth and dimensions of the carvings in *Reims* may only be compared with that of Greek sculpture. Head of Joseph (c. 1260).

Ein halbes Jahrhundert vor dem Josef von Reims entstand die asketische Figur Johannes d. T. vom mittleren Westportal in *Chartres* (1200–1210).

The ascetic figure of John the Baptist of the West Portal in *Chartres* (1200–1210), carved half a century before the head of Joseph at Reims.

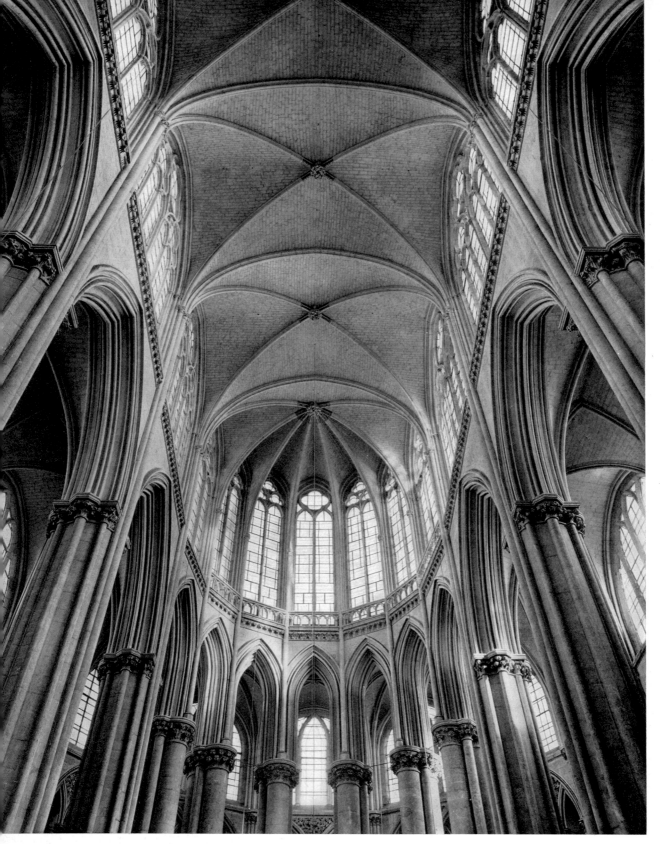

Foto Marburg

Dem Einstrom flutenden Lichtes offen! Der 1217 begonnene, 33 m hohe Chor von *Le Mans* ist eine der edelsten Schöpfungen gotischer Baukunst.

The 108 ft. high choir of *Le Mans* flooded in light. Begun in 1217, it is one of the finest creations of Gothic architecture.

Le Mans. Die Außenseite dieses Chores zeigt, welches tektonische Gerüst notwendig ist, um solche äußerste Durchlichtung des Raumes zu ermöglichen.

Le Mans. This view of the exterior shows what structural ingenuity is required to allow such penetration of light into the choir.

Die Portalplastik von *Amiens* (um 1230) steht zeitlich zwischen
der von Chartres und Reims – mit beiden zusammen ist sie
allenthalben in Europa zum Vorbild geworden. Apostel vom Westportal.

The portals of *Amiens* (c. 1230) were carved at some time between
those of Chartres and Reims. The sculptures of these three cathedrals
were an inspiration everywhere in Europe. Apostles from the West Portal.

Jeite

Die 1225–1235 entstandene Westfassade von *Amiens* mit der im 15. Jh
in spätgotischer Formensprache erneuerten Maßwerkfüllung der Rose

The West Front of *Amiens* (1225–1235). The tracery of the ros
window was renewed in the 15th century in the Late Gothic style

Unter den klassischen
französischen Kathedralen
besticht die von *Amiens* durch
Eleganz des Aufbaus und
warme Lebensfülle ihrer
Westfassade.

Amiens stands out among the
classic French cathedrals by
the elegance of its structure
and the warmth of the
West Front.

Das schlanke Mittelschiff
(1220–1236) der Kathedrale
von *Amiens* mit der starken
Betonung ihrer Vertikalen.

The slender nave (1200–1236)
of *Amiens* Cathedral with its
strong emphasis on the
vertical.

Der *Kölner* Dom (beg. 1248, vollendet im 19. Jh.)
ist die Verwandlung französischer
Baugedanken in deutschen Ausdruckswillen.
Links: Der triumphierenden Aufwärtsbewegung der
Türme ordnen sich die Portale unter.
Rechts: Das schluchtartige Innere, konsequente
Weiterentwicklung des Innenraums von Amiens.

Cologne Cathedral (begun 1248, completed 19th ct.)
is a German expression of French
architectural theories. Left: the portals subordinate
themselves to the triumphant upward surge of the
towers. Right: the gorge-like interior is a
consistent further development of that of Amiens.

53

Man hat gotische Pfeiler den Aposteln verglichen, welche die Kirche tragen. — Die 27 m hohen Bündelpfeiler des *Kölner* Doms.

Gothic piers have been compared to the apostles bearing the Church. The 89 ft piers of *Cologne* Cathedral with their clustered shafts.

Seeger-Müller

Wandgliederung der Kathedrale von *Beauvais* (1272) — des gewaltigsten, Torso gebliebenen Unternehmens gotischen Kathedralbaus.
Bay-formation at *Beauvais* Cathedral (1272), the mightiest of Gothic undertakings, still towerless.

Jeiter

Das unirdische, „gotische" Lächeln des Engels der Verkündigung vom Mittelportal der Kathedrale in *Reims* (um 1250/60).

The ethereal „Gothic" smile of the Angel Gabriel in the Annunciation, centre portal of *Reims* Cathedral (c. 1250—1260).

Hochgotische Plastik in Deutschland. Maria und Christus, die gleichsam vom Bewegungsstrom der Architektur durchrauschten Pfeilerfiguren im *Kölner* Dom.

High Gothic sculpture in Germany. Mary and Christ, figures carved on the piers of *Cologne* Cathedral, are inspired by the architectural flow of movement.

Chor des Doms zu *Köln*. Die reich
durchbrochene Wandfläche wird
durch die Glasbildfenster zum Ein-
fallstor der überirdischen
Glaubenswelt.

The choir of *Cologne* Cathedral.
Through the many stained glass
windows which divide up the wall
we get our first glimpse of the
spiritual world.

Stursberg →

Am reinsten offenbart sich die
Tendenz, Wandflächen durch Fenster
zu ersetzen, in der Sainte Chapelle
zu *Paris* (um 1250).

The Ste. Chapelle in *Paris* (c. 1250)
reveals most clearly the tendency to
eliminate the whole wall by
substituting windows.

Gotische Glasmalerei nimmt zuweilen
die zeitgenössische Plastik zum Vorbild.
Das ältere Marienfenster, Elisabethkirche
zu *Marburg*.

Gothic stained glass was often inspired
by contemporary sculpture. The earlier
St. Mary Window in the Elisabethkirche
Marburg.

Busch

Busch →

Meist aber ist das gotische Glasbild eine
teppichhafte Folge von Szenerien.
Das Fenster mit der Jugendgeschichte
Christi im Münster zu *Straßburg*.

A series of scenes are usually depicted,
not unlike tapestry, on the stained glass.
Window illustrating the youth of Christ,
Strasbourg Cathedral.

Franz. Kulturdienst

Jeiter

Der *Mont St. Michel* auf einem Granitfelsen vor der normannischen
Küste, eine Burg Gottes im Reich der Gezeiten (10. bis 13. Jh.).

Mont St. Michel on a granite rock off the coast of Normandy,
a sea-swept monastery (10th–13th centuries).

Der Burgberg des *Mont St. Michel*, gesehen von dem zum Festland
führenden Damm aus.

The rock of *Mont St. Michel* taken from the causeway leading
to the mainland.

Foto Marburg

Mont St. Michel. Der 1228 veränderte,
höchst dekorative Kreuzgang des Klosters.

Mont St. Michel. The highly decorative
cloisters of the monastery, altered in 1228.

Englische Gotik gestaltet flächiger und dekorativer als die französische.
Engelschor (1256–1320) der Kathedrale von *Lincoln*, ein früher Glanzpunkt des „Decorated Style".

English Gothic is more "solid" and decorative than French. Angel Choir (1256–1320) of *Lincoln* Cathedral,
a splendid early example of the Decorated Style.

Felton ⟶

Foto Marburg

Eine statische Notwendigkeit wird freimütig zur Schau gestellt:
Innenverstrebungen unter dem Vierungsturm
der Kathedrale von *Salisbury*.

The need to counter the inward thrust of the flying buttresses found
expression in the "girders" across the eastern transept of
Salisbury Cathedral.

Hochaltar, östliche Vierung und Chor (1269) der Westminster Abbe
in *London*, Schauplatz der historischen Zeremonie
im englischen Königreich

High altar, eastern crossing and choir (126
of Westminster Abbey in *Londo*
scene of many historic ceremonie

Felte

Wesenhaft englisch – die in ihrem
Hauptteil 1220–1266 erbaute
Kathedrale von *Salisbury*.
Der Hauptturm (beg. 1334) ragt
über der Vierung auf, die Fassade
ist mit nebeneinandergereihten
Bildwerken überzogen.

Salisbury Cathedral –
built 1220–1266 – is typically English.
The central tower (begun 1334)
rises between the north and south
transepts, the façade is decorated
with rows of statues.

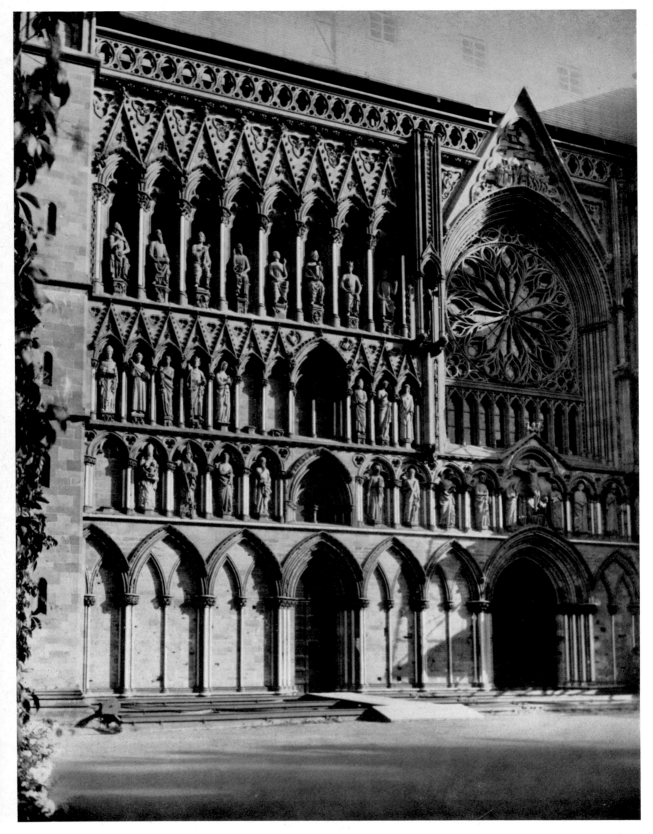

larsen

Der Nidaros-Dom, *Drontheim* in Norwegen, ist die größte Kirche Skandinaviens. Rein gotisch sind das Schiff (1232—48) und die Westfassade (im Bild), die starke Beziehungen zu englischen Bauten aufweist.

Nidaros Cathedral at *Trondhjem* in Norway is the largest church in Scandinavia. The nave (1232—48) and the West Front (in photograph) are Gothic, the latter showing strong English influences.

70

Kersting

Eines der schönsten Bilder englischer Frühgotik, des „Early English", bietet die auf grünem Anger gelegene Kathedrale von *Wells*. Die als Schmuckwand gedachte Westfassade (1220—39) breitet in 350 Figuren den bedeutendsten Zyklus englischer Plastik aus.

Wells Cathedral, set in a green Close, presents one of the most beautiful pictures of Early Gothic. The 350 statues on the ornamental wall of the West Front (1220—39) form the most important cycle of sculptured figures in England.

71

Felton

Felton →

Die Vierung der Dreifaltigkeitskathedrale in *Ely* mit der Phantastik ihres hölzernen Sterngewölbes, das 1342 nach dem Einsturz des romanischen Vierungsturmes konstruiert wurde.

The crossing of the Cathedral Church of the Holy and Undivided Trinity in *Ely,* with its marvellous timber star-vaulting, carried out in 1342 after the collapse of the Norman central tower.

Ein Beispiel aus der Zeit des „Dekorativen Stiles" – die St. Peters Kathedrale in *Exeter* mit dem berauschenden Linienspiel der Gewölbe, Pfeiler, Galerien und Zierate.

An example of the Decorated Style, St. Peter's Cathedral in *Exeter,* with the dazzling interplay of lines to be found in vaults, piers, triforium and ornaments.

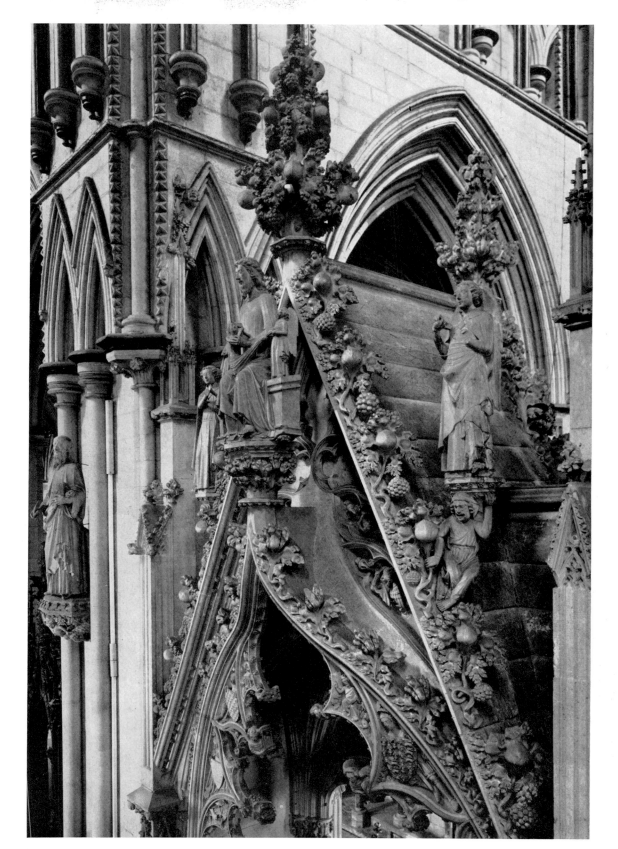

Die Westfassade
(um 1280 beg.) der
Kathedrale von *Lichfield*
in England steht durch
die ungegliederte
Reihung von Figuren
und die geringe
Betonung der Portale
im krassen Gegensatz
zur französischen
Kathedralarchitektur.

The West Front
(1280 seqq.) of *Lichfield*
Cathedral in England
with its regular
tiers of statues and the
scant emphasis on the
portals presents a sharp
contrast to French
cathedral architecture.

Der Chor (1225–1245) des Münsters von *Beverley* birgt das spätgotische Percy-Grabmal
mit seinem wuchernden Schmuck von sogen. Kriechblumen.

The choir (1225–45) of *Beverley* Minster, with the Late Gothic Percy Tomb, a riot of stone creepers.

Foto Marburg

Englische Hochgotik des „Decorated Style".
Das 1233 eingewölbte Langhaus der Kathedrale von *Lincoln* besitzt Dekorationen von einem besonderen Reichtum der Details.

English High Gothic in the Decorated Style.
The nave of *Lincoln* Cathedral, vaulted in 1233, boasts an incomparable wealth of ornamental detail.

Felton

Noch spätromanisch-normannisch im Unterbau der Türme,
entstand die breitgelagerte Kathedrale von *Lincoln* in den gotischen Teilen der Westfassade um 1220–1230.

The lower ranges of the twin towers are of Late Romanesque arcading,
but the Gothic parts of the West Façade of sprawling *Lincoln* Cathedral date from c. 1220–1230.

Die Kathedrale von *Bristol* (Anf. 14. Jh.) verkörpert in England die „Wendung zum Einheitsraum" des Hallenkirchentypus.
In konsequenter Fortführung der Baugedanken ist das Gewölbe des Südquerschiffs höchst eigenwillig gestaltet.

Bristol Cathedral (early 14th century) illustrates the change towards a unified room of the aisled hall type.
For technical reasons, nave and aisles being of equal height, a highly individual type of vaulting was used in the south transept.

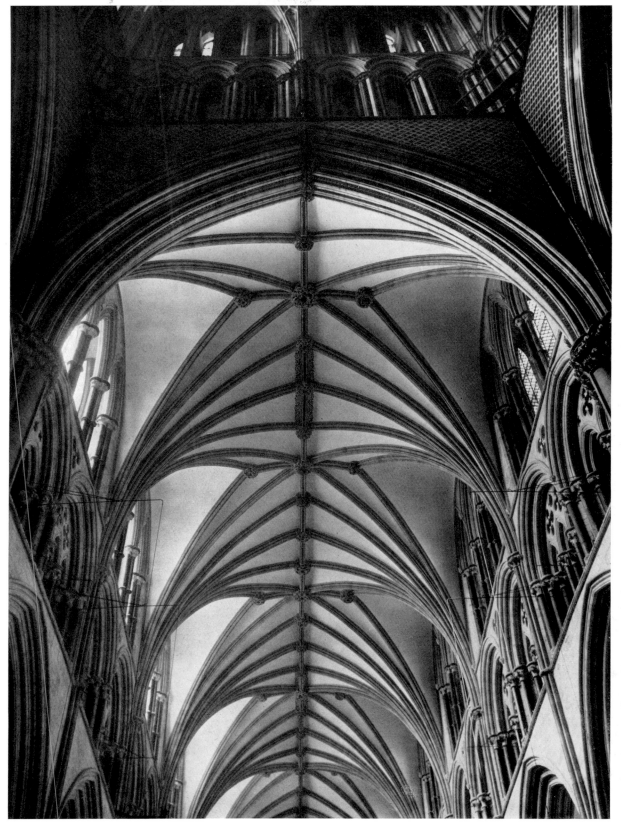

Die Kathedrale von *Lincoln* zeigt in den 7 Jochen des Mittelschiffs den ersten Versuch zu einer reicheren Ausstattung der Gewölbe.
Deutlich wird die bindende Aufgabe der Scheitelrippe.

At *Lincoln* Cathedral a first experiment in more decorative vaulting was made in the seven bays of the nave connected by a ridge rib.
This special English form of vault is also known as the keel-vault.

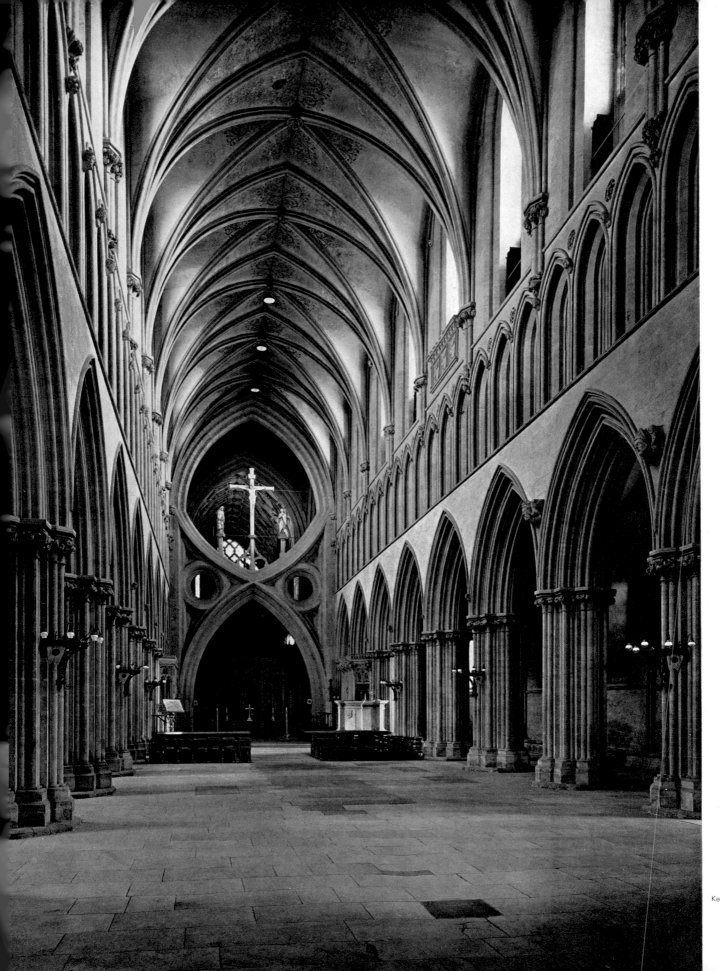

Wells. Links: Blick aus dem Mittelschiff (1192—1230) gegen die Vierung nach Osten. Oben: Die phantastische Geometrie verstrebender Bögen unter dem Vierungsturm (1338) macht aus einer tektonischen Notwendigkeit ein künstlerisches Ausdrucksmittel.

Wells. View taken from the nave (1192—1230) of the crossing looking eastwards (left). Two typical features of English Gothic — the emphasis on horizontals achieved by the triforium with its long line of arcades, and the geometry of supporting arches (above) — mark the crossing (1338).

Schwergelagerte Kuben, aufgelockert durch Blendbögen: der Papstpalast
in *Avignon*, der den römischen Oberhirten 1334—1352 als Exil diente.

Heavy cubes relieved by ornamental arches: the Palace of the Popes in
Avignon, home of the exiled pontiffs from 1334—1352.

„Irische Akropolis" nennt man die auf dem Felsen von *Cashe*
emporragende Ruine der im 13. Jh. angelegten Kathedrale

The 13th century cathedral ruins towering above the rock of *Cashe*
have been termed the "Irish Acropolis"

Busch

Der prachtvolle Saalbau (um 1280) des Landgrafenschlosses in *Marburg* an der Lahn, einer der wenigen künstlerisch gestalteten weltlichen Bauten der hohen Gotik.

The hall building (c. 1280) of the Landgraves' Castle in *Marburg* on the Lahn, one of the few really artistic secular buildings of the High Gothic period.

Im Saalbau des *Marburger* Schlosses. Mit Dehio kann man hier von einem „monumentalen Idealismus" auch der weltlichen Baugesinnung sprechen.

The hall of *Marburg* Castle. Like Dehio, we can speak of a "monumental idealism" even in secular architecture.

Schmidt-Glaßner

Das reiche Isabella-Grabmal, eines der schönsten gotischen Grabmäler überhaupt,
im Chorumgang der Zisterzienserklosterkirche von *Alcobaça* (1158–1223), Portugal.

The lavishly carved Isabella Monument, one of the finest Gothic tombs in existence,
from the Cistercian conventual church of *Alcobaça* (1158–1223) in Portugal.

86

Echagüe

An Schönheit und Größe kaum übertroffen: das frühgotische Refektorium des 1142 gegründeten Klosters *Santa Maria de la Huerta* (Soria) in Spanien. Schon früh ist die Gotik mit den Zisterziensern auf die iberische Halbinsel gekommen.

Unsurpassable in beauty and dimensions: the Early Gothic refectory of the Monastery of *Santa Maria de la Huerta* (Soria) in Spain. It was the Cistercians who introduced Gothic to the Iberian Peninsula at an early date.

Der Ausgestaltung ihrer Kapitelhäuser wendeten die großen Mönchsorden besondere Sorgfalt zu.
Oben: *Maulbronn*, das erste Netzgewölbe in Deutschland. Rechts: Palmettengewölbe, *Salisbury* (um 1280).

The great monastic orders devoted special attention to the embellishment of their chapter-houses.
Above: *Maulbronn*, the earliest net-vaulting to be found in Germany. Right: palm-vaulting at *Salisbury* (c. 1280).

Fast ein Übermaß an Rippen überzieht die Gewölbe im achteckigen Kapitelhaus (1319 vollendet) der Kathedrale von *Wells*.

A profusion of rib-vaulting characterises the octagonal chapter-house of *Wells* (completed in 1319).

Der große Remter im Hochmeisterpalast der *Marienburg* an der Nogat mit seinem herrlichen Palmettengewölbe von 1320.

The great refectory in the High Master's Palace at *Marienburg* on the Nogat, with its splendid palm-vaulting (1320).

Wagner

Eine der bedeutendsten Kirchen Skandinaviens ist die Kathedrale von *Linköping* (um 1260) in Schweden.
Ein Hallenkirchentyp, wie er in Westfalen und im Poitou zuerst ausgebildet wurde.

Linköping Cathedral (c. 1260) in Sweden is one of the most important churches in Scandinavia.
It is of the "hall-church" type, first perfected in Westphalia and Poitou.

Die von einem englischen König gestiftete Kathedrale in *Poitiers* (1170–90)
ist mit ihren zeltähnlichen Kuppelgewölben ein echter Hallenbau. Mittelschiff gegen Osten.

Poitiers Cathedral (1170–90), endowed by Henry II of England,
is a genuine "hall-church" with its tent-like dome-vault. Nave looking east.

Busch

Das früheste reingotische Gotteshaus Deutschlands, zugleich seine erste gotische Hallenkirche:
die Elisabethkirche in *Marburg* (beg. 1235). Blick vom Chor nach Westen.

The earliest purely Gothic "hall-church" in Germany: the Elisabethkirche in *Marburg* (1235 seqq.).
View from the choir westwards.

Busch

Elisabethkirche in *Marburg*. Der Triumphbogen über dem hochgotischen Lettner, seiner Figuren beraubt —
aber noch immer im überreichen Schmuck seines Laubwerkes prangend.

The Elisabethkirche in *Marburg*. The triumphal arch over the High Gothic rood-screen,
bereft of its statues but still richly decked in foliage.

Aufsberg

Der eigenartige Rundbau eines Heiligen Grabes im Münster zu *Konstanz* ist, in kleinem Maßstab, die Verwirklichung der freischöpferischen Bauphantasie eines unbekannten Meisters.

The strange circular construction of a Holy Sepulchre in *Constance* Cathedral is, on a small scale, the realisation of an unknown architect's dreams.

Schmidt-Glaßner

Die Liebfrauenkirche in *Trier*, ein im Innern wundervoll leichter Zentralbau (1242 begonnen).
Die im Bild rechts sichtbaren Türme gehören dem benachbarten Dom an.

The Liebfrauenkirche in *Treves* (1242 seqq.) which has a wonderfully light and airy interior.
The two towers visible to the right form part of the neighbouring cathedral.

Deutschland löst sich nur schwer vom romanischen Baustil. Das südliche Seitenschiff (um 1256)
der Hallenkirche des *Mindener* Domes mit einem der Fenster, deren Maßwerk an romanische
Radfenster erinnert.

Germany found it hard to break away from the Romanesque. The south transept (c. 1256)
of *Minden* Cathedral ("hall-church" type) with one of the windows, the tracery of which
resembles that of a Romanesque wheel-window.

Die lichteste aller gotischen
Hallenkirchen ist die
zeltartig leichte Kirche
Maria zur Wiese (um 1350)
in *Soest*, deren Pfeiler
ohne Kapitelle in die
Gewölbe übergehen.

The brightest of all Gothic
"hall-churches" is the
tent-like Maria zur Wiese
(c. 1350) in *Soest*,
Westphalia, the piers
of which shoot straight up to
the vault without capitals.

99   Busch

Zwei Beispiele skulpturengeschmückter Kapitelle. Oben: *Reims*, Kapitell eines Pfeilers mit der Darstellung der Weinernte. Unten: Elisabethkirche in *Marburg*, Pfeilerkapitell mit sparsam gestreutem Weinlaub.

Two examples of sculptured capitals. Above: *Reims*, capital representing the grape-harvest. Below: Elisabethkirche in *Marburg*, capital carved with sparsely-strewn vine leaves.

Ein Kennzeichen gotischer Wandmalerei des 13. Jh. ist die dienende Einordnung der zeichnerisch empfundenen Malerei in die Architektur. St. Maria Lyskirchen, *Köln:* Nikolauslegende (1250—1260).

Gothic mural-painting of the 13th century, with its draughtsman-like quality unrelated to space, harmonises with the architecture. *Cologne:* legend of St. Nicholas (1250—1260).

101

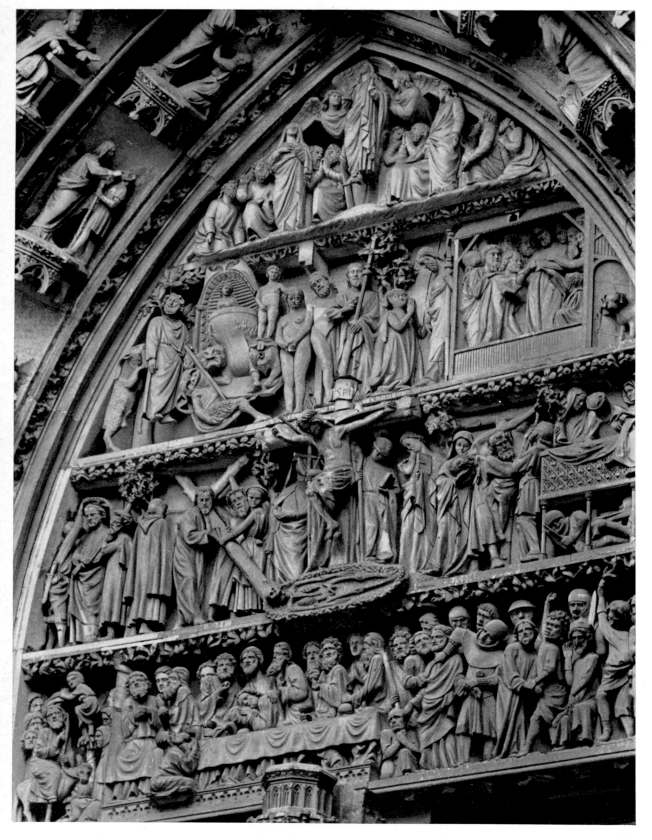

Jeiter

Der heilsgeschichtliche Zyklus, den die romanische Epoche auf Wandbildern im Innern der Gotteshäuser darstellte, wird jetzt zum großen Thema plastischer Portalkunst. *Straßburger* Münster: Tympanon des Mittelportales (um 1280).

The cycle of figures depicting the Redemption to be found during the Romanesque period inside the church is now transferred to the portals. *Strasbourg* Cathedral: tympanum of the centre portal (c. 1280).

Foto Marburg

Die gotische Epoche entdeckt die Schönheit der irdischen Welt. An Stelle eines Figurenreliefs überzieht Rankenwerk das Tympanon des Westportals der *Marburger* Elisabethkirche. Auch in den Türbeschlägen kehrt das Pflanzenmotiv wieder.

The Gothic period discovers the beauty of the earthly world. Instead of a figure-relief, foliage decorates the tympanum of the West Portal of the Elisabethkirche at *Marburg*. The same motif recurs in the wrought-ironwork on the door.

Busch

Das *Straßburger* Münster besitzt in der „Harfenbespannung" der unteren Partien der Westfront (links) mit den vielen Skulpturen (1276—1300) die vielleicht schönste gotische Fassade. Oben: Fürst der Welt und Törichte Jungfrauen vom südlichen Westportal.

Strasbourg with the so-called "harp-stringing" on the lower parts of the richly carved West Front (left) has perhaps the finest Gothic façade of any cathedral. Above: The Prince of Darkness and Foolish Virgins from the West Portal.

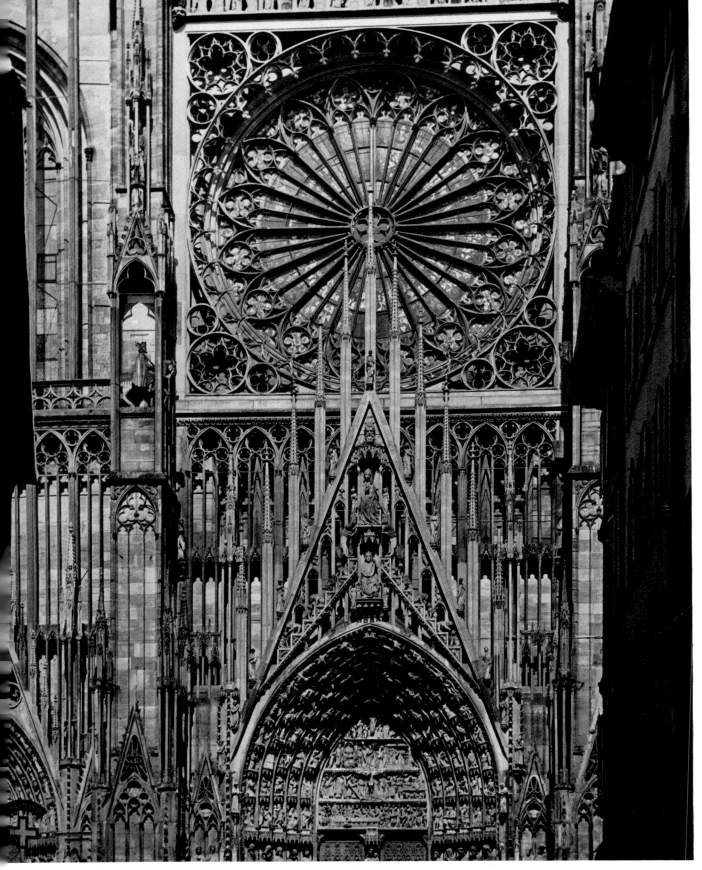

Busch

Bis zum Rosenfenster ist die Westfassade des *Straßburger* Domes nach dem einzigartigen Entwurf Meister Erwins von Steinbach geschaffen worden.
The West Façade of *Strasbourg* Cathedral, including the great rose-window, was built according to the unique plan of Master Erwin of Steinbach.

Straßburg. Eine virtuosenhaft kühle Kunst übte der Meister, der die Prophetenfiguren vom Gewände des mittleren Westportals schuf.

Strasbourg. The master who created the figures of the Prophets on the jamb of the centre West Portal was a virtuoso.

Eine der schönsten Turmschöpfungen gotischer Kunst
ist unzweifelhaft das Steinfiligran
des *Freiburger* Münsterturmes (um 1350).

One of the most beautiful towers of Gothic art
is undoubtedly the stone-filigree spire
of *Freiburg* Minster (c. 1350).

Seeger-Müller ⟶

In zahlreichen Bauetappen ist im Laufe
von vier Jahrhunderten nach wechselnden Plänen
das *Straßburger* Münster emporgewachsen.

Strasbourg Cathedral was constructed by stages
in the course of four centuries
according to changing plans.

Die noch aus magischem Bewußtsein stammenden Dämonen
sind in „aufgeklärterer", gotischer Zeit
zu grotesken Wasserspeiern geworden. *Freiburger* Münster.

The demons, originally thought to have magic properties,
became in the "enlightened" Gothic age grotesque gargoyles.
Freiburg Minster.

Die lehrhafte Rolle der gotischen Bauplastik
spricht aus den Figuren des Höllenfürsten und der Voluptas
in der *Freiburger* Münstervorhalle (um 1310).

The instructive rôle of Gothic sculpture
can be seen from the figures of the Prince of Hell and Voluptas
in the porch of *Freiburg* Minster (c. 1310).

110

Foto Marburg

Roubier

Klassischer französischer Figurenstil:
Auferstehende vom Westportal der Kathedrale von *Bourges*.

Classic French style:
figures rising from the dead, West Portal of *Bourges* Cathedral.

Expressiv deutsch in der Gebärdensprache: Die Törichten Jungfrauen
vom Nordwestportal der *Erfurter* Marienkirche (um 1360).

The Foolish Virgins from the North-West Portal of the Marienkirche
in *Erfurt* (c. 1360), typically German in gesture and bearing.

113

Was die Kathedrale von *Bourges* (beg. 1192) so bedeutend macht, die großartige Verbindung südlichen Raumempfindens mit nördlicher Emporbewegung, scheint sich auch in dem breitausladenden Christusportal auszudrücken.

In *Bourges* Cathedral (1192 seqq.) one finds combined the upward thrust characteristic of northern Gothic and the feeling of space encountered in the south. The wide Christ Portal.

114

Refot

Dem Stile französischer Kathedralen folgt die von Etienne de Bonneuil, einem der französischen Mitarbeiter von Notre Dame in Paris, geschaffene Domkyrka (1270–1315) im schwedischen *Upsala*. Langhaus gegen den Chor.

The Domkyrka (1270–1315) in *Upsala*, Sweden, created by Etienne de Bonneuil, one of the architects of Notre Dame, copies the style of French cathedrals. Nave looking towards the choir.

Schneiders

Mit dem Ausgang der großen Zeit deutscher Kaiser
ewinnt die französische Baukunst an Einfluß. Das Südportal (1269—1279)
er Ritterstiftskirche in *Wimpfen*, ein „opus francigenum".

he decline of the German Emperors saw the increase
f French architectural influences. The South Portal (1269—1279)
f the Ritterstiftskirche in *Wimpfen*.

Obere Partie des Seitenschiffes
der Zisterzienserkirche von *Haina* in Hessen,
die in der Nachfolge der Marburger Elisabethkirche entstand.

Upper part of the aisle
in the Cistercian church of *Haina* in Hesse,
inspired by the Elisabethkirche, Marburg.

17

Voller Kraft des Ausdrucks: die formenreiche und zugleich strenge Westfassade des Klosters *Chorin* in der Mark Brandenburg (1334), eines der erlauchtesten Beispiele gotischer Backsteinarchitektur.

The West Façade of *Chorin* Monastery in Brandenburg (1334), forceful, expressive, severe yet shapely in design, is one of the most illustrious examples of Brick Gothic.

Schneiders

Den alten Baugedanken der von einem Umgang umzogenen Apsis, freilich mit den Mitteln der Backsteinarchitektur, nimmt die Kathedrale von *Roskilde* (beg. um 1215) in Dänemark auf.

The old theory of an apse surrounded by an ambulatory is carried out in brickwork at the cathedral of *Roskilde* (c. 1215 seqq.) in Denmark.

Mitte des 14. Jh. hat sich die Gotik bereits bis tief hinein nach Polen ausgebreitet.
In der um 1360 von Meister Peter geschaffenen Marienkirche in *Krakau:* der Chor mit dem Triumphkreuz aus der Werkstatt des Veit Stoß.

By the mid-14th century, Gothic had already spread as far afield as Poland.
The Church of St. Mary in *Cracow,* created by Master Peter in 1360, with the triumphal cross from Veit Stoss' workshop.

120

Das Innere der
Lübecker Marienkirche,
die zum großen Vorbild
im Ostseebereich
geworden ist.
Blick gegen den
zwischen 1251 und 1291
erbauten Chor.

The interior of the
Marienkirche, *Lübeck*,
an inspiration to
Baltic architects.
View of the choir
constructed between
1251 and 1291.

Castelli

Die Kathedrale von *York* (Ende 13. bis 15. Jh.)
st in ihrer Weitläufigkeit und der Betonung des Vierungsturmes
ine charakteristisch englische Anlage.

ork Minster (late 13th — 15th century),
s typically English in its sprawling plan and emphasis
n the central tower and crossing.

Die kreuzförmige Basilika des Stephansdomes
in *Halberstadt* (13. bis 15. Jh.) — beispielhaft für die Gesamtanlage
einer gotischen Kathedrale in Deutschland.

The cruciform basilica of the Stephansdom
in *Halberstadt* (13th — 15th century) — typical of the general plan
of a German Gothic cathedral.

Schmidt-Glaßner

Das ausgesprochen gotische Stadtbild von *Erfurt*
mit den Kirchen St. Marien und St. Severi.

A decidedly Gothic scene: the town of *Erfurt*
with the churches of St. Marien and St. Severi.

Ulm. Turm des Münsters, zwar erst im 19. Jh. entstanden,
aber in seinem Aufbau nach einem alten Plan doch den Geist der Gotik atmend.

Ulm. The 19th century Minster spire, built in accordance
with an old plan, is still in keeping with the spirit of Gothic.

Normannisch-englischer Einfluß zeigt sich in vielen Kirchen der Bretagne.
Links: S. Corentin im Stadtbild von *Quimper* (Turmspitzen 19. Jh.). Unten: S. Tugdual zu *Tréguier* (beg. 1339).

Norman influences from England are reflected in many Breton churches.
Left: St. Corentin in the heart of *Quimper* (19th ct. spire). Below: St. Tugdual at *Tréguier* (1339 seqq.).

← Halbach

Die schlichte, turmlose
Zisterzienserkirche
zu *Altenberg*
im Rheinland (beg. 1255).
Das schmückende
riesige Westfenster
aus späterer Zeit
(nach 1379).

The plain, towerless
Cistercian church
of Altenberg in the
Rhineland (1255 seqq.).
The huge, decorative
West Front dates from a
later period (post 1379).

Die konsequente Auflösung
der Wandflächen in Fenster:
der *Aachener* Münsterchor
(beg. 1355).

The consistent merging
of wall into window:
the cathedral choir
(c. 1355 seqq.)
in *Aix-la-Chapelle*.

129   Busch

Der nach 1300 einsetzende Wandel der Baugesinnung spricht aus der Schmuckfülle des Maßwerks.
Nürnberg, St. Lorenz.

The rich ornamental tracery of St. Lorenz, *Nuremberg,* is indicative of the change
in architectural style introduced after 1300.

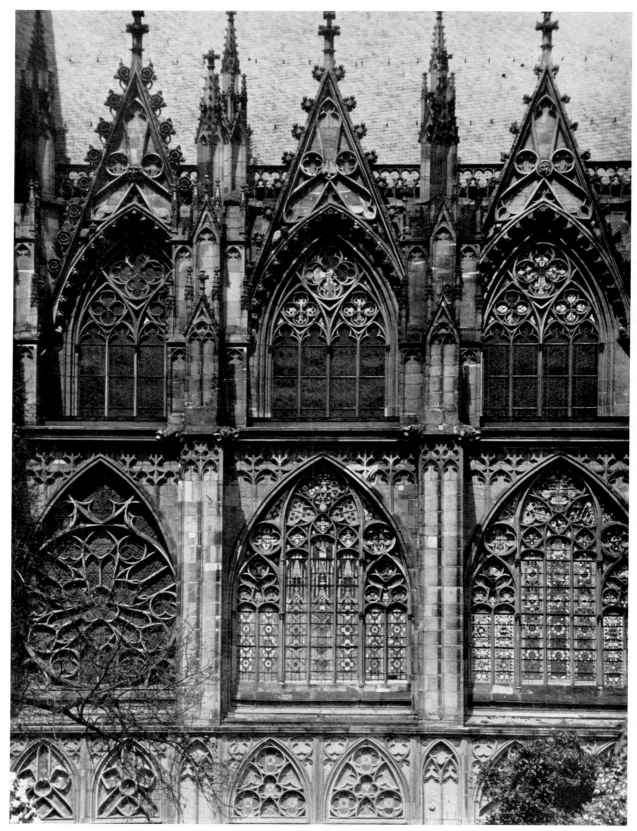

H. Retzlaff

Wie ein Nebenstück zur Nürnberger Rose wirken die besonders reichen Maßwerkfenster an der Südwand der Katharinenkirche in *Oppenheim* am Rhein (um 1320—1340).

The exceptional richness of the window-tracery on the south wall of the Katharinenkirche, *Oppenheim* (c. 1320—1340), vividly recalls that of the rose-window in Nuremberg.

Aufsberg

Bewußt schlicht gehalten sind die gotischen Kirchen der Bettelorden.
Zumal in Italien wird ihr Charakter als Predigtkirche deutlich. San Francesco, *Assisi* (gegr. 1228).

There is a studied simplicity about the Gothic churches of the Mendicants.
Their special character — that of a preaching hall — is particularly apparent in Italy. San Francesco, *Assisi* (founded 1228).

132

Der schlichte, klare Raum von Sta. Maria Novella zu *Florenz* (beg. 1278) läßt trotz gotischer
Formen schon das Raumgefühl der Frührenaissance ahnen.

Despite its Gothic forms, the plain, clear interior of Sta. Maria Novella in *Florence*
(post 1278) seems to herald the early Renaissance in its attitude to space.

133

H. Retzlaff

In Italien wird das französische Vorbild, der feingegliederte Organismus der gotischen Kathedrale,
zum festen Block mit harmonischen Flächenbegrenzungen abgewandelt. S. Maria della Spina, *Pisa* (1230—1323).

In Italy, the French model — the delicately jointed organism of the Gothic cathedral —
is transformed into a solid block of harmonious character. S. Maria della Spina, *Pisa* (1230—1323).

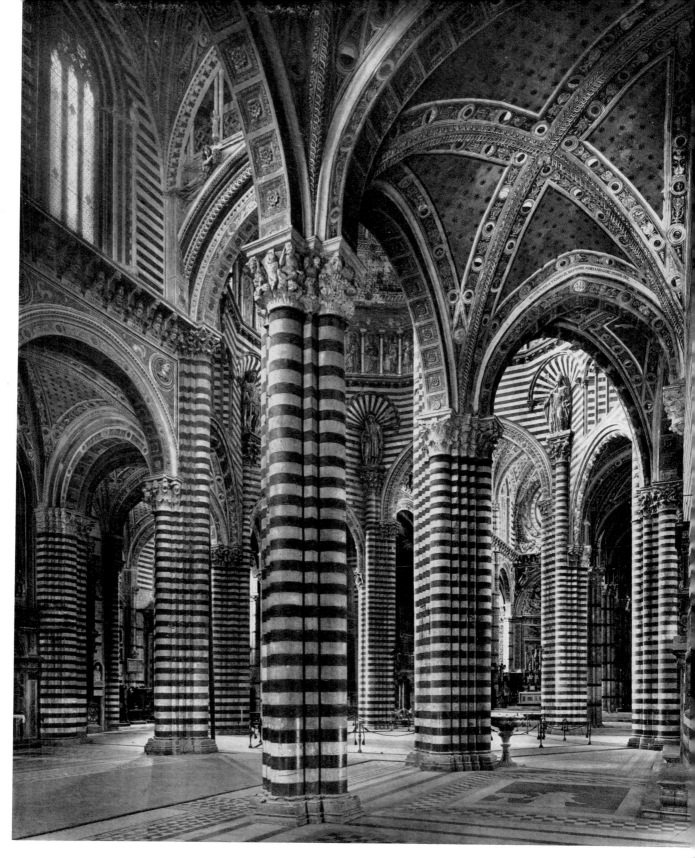

Der Raumeindruck der italienischen Kirchen wird meist von einer Vierungskuppel bestimmt.
Siena, Dom. Blick aus dem Seitenschiff (vollendet 1264).

The impression of space in Italian churches is mostly determined by the central cupola.
Siena Cathedral. View from the aisle (completed in 1264).

Brogi

Eine der größten unter den wenigen italienischen Kirchen von spürbar gotischem Geist:
St. Petronio in *Bologna* (1390—1430).

One of the greatest of the few Italian churches which are clearly Gothic in spirit:
San Petronio in *Bologna* (1390—1430).

Ein bezeichnendes Werk italienischer Bauplastik aus der Zeit der Wende zwischen Gotik und Renaissance: das Tabernakel (1349–1359) von Andrea Orcagna im Bethaus der Zünfte Or San Michele zu *Florenz*.

A characteristic work of Italian sculpture from the transition period between Gothic and Renaissance: Andrea Orcagna's Tabernacle (1349–1359) in the chapel of the Guilds, Or San Michele, *Florence*.

Jeiter

Palma de Mallorca. Oben: Die wehrhafte, durch zahlreiche Strebepfeiler fast flächig wirkende Südseite der Kathedrale.
Rechts: Das Innere der Kathedrale, die das Hauptbeispiel der katalanischen, die Raumweite betonenden Gotik ist (Anfang 14. Jh.).

Palma, Majorca. Above: buttressing on the south side of the fortress-like cathedral.
Right: interior, the principal example of Catalan Gothic with its emphasis on breadth (early 14th century).

Die Franziskaner und Dominikaner haben in Italien den Kirchenstil der Saalkirche geschaffen. Santa Croce (gegr. 1294) in *Florenz*.

The Franciscans and Dominicans developed in Italy the church style of the plain hall. Santa Croce in *Florence* (founded 1294).

Roubier

Einer Backsteinfestung gleicht die Kathedrale von *Albi* (1282–1365), ein Beispiel katalanischer Bauweise in Südfrankreich.
Albi Cathedral (1282–1365), an example of the Catalan architectural style which spread to S. France, looks like a brick fortress.

Kerff

Castel del Monte in Apulien (um 1240),
das Jagdschloß des Hohenstaufenkaisers Friedrich II.,
verbindet die Mächtigkeit der Romanik mit gotischen Baugedanken.

The tremendous force of Romanesque and the building theories of Gothic
are combined in *Castel del Monte* in Apulia (c. 1240),
the hunting-seat of the Hohenstaufen Emperor Frederick II.

Jaime II. hat die runde Burg Bellver bei *Palma de Mallorca* im 13. Jh.
anlegen lassen, deren schönster Teil der Innenhof mit der Galerie ist.

Jaime II instigated the building of the cylindrical 13th ct. Castle of Bellver
near *Palma, Majorca*. The finest part is the inner courtyard with gallery.

Jeiter

Das Stadtschloß Grafenstein in *Gent* (ab 1180), stolze Erinnerung an das Rittertum der gotischen Epoche.

Gravensteen Castle in *Ghent* (c. 1180), a proud reminder of chivalry during the Gothic period.

144

Die Anlage gotischer Burgen entspricht meist weniger künstlerischen als praktischen Bedürfnissen.
Einige dieser Bauten beeindrucken jedoch nicht nur durch ihre Lage und blockartigen Mauern. *Conway Castle* in Wales.

Gothic castles were in most cases planned in accordance with practical rather than with artistic needs.
In some cases, however, they are impressive not only on account of their commanding situation and massive walls. *Conway Castle* in Wales.

145

Das gotische Bauviertel von *Barcelona* innerhalb der heutigen Altstadt.
Die Stadt war um 1470 das am dichtesten bevölkerte Gemeinwesen der Pyrenäenhalbinsel.

The Gothic quarter of *Barcelona* in the old part of the town.
Around 1470 it was the most densely populated town of the Peninsula.

Wegener

Schloß und Dom von *Marienwerder* in der Weichselniederung (1300—1384),
neben der Marienburg die bekannteste aller Wehranlagen des Deutschen Ordens.

The castle and cathedral of *Marienwerder* in the plain of the Vistula (1300—1384),
after the Marienburg the best-known of all fortresses owned by the Teutonic Knights.

Aerofilms Ltd.

Busch

Stokesay Castle in Shropshire, England, ein um 1291 befestigter Adelssitz . . .

Stokesay Castle in Shropshire, England, fortified in 1291 . . .

. . und eine deutsche Wohnburg, die trotz ihrer langen Baugeschichte ihren wehrhaft-geschlossenen Charakter aus gotischer Zeit bewahrt hat. *Burg Eltz* in einem Seitental der unteren Mosel.

. . and a German castle which has preserved its defensive "Gothic" character although centuries elapsed before its completion. *Eltz Castle* in a valley adjoining the Lower Moselle.

150

Alinar

Zeichen des Bürgerbewußtseins der zur Führung gekommenen Städte — die Türme der gotischen Rat- und Zunfthäuser.
Links: Die „Hallen" in *Brügge* (2. Hälfte 13. Jh.) mit dem 85 m hohen Belfried.
Oben: Das im 13. Jh. nach italienischer Art kastenförmig erbaute Rathaus, der Palazzo dei Priori in *Volterra.*

The towers of the Gothic townhalls and guildhalls are an indication of the awakening of a civic consciousness.
Left: the "Hallas" in *Bruges* (late 13th century) with the 279 ft. belfry.
Above: the townhall of the Palazzo dei Priori in *Volterra,* built in the box-like Italian manner of the 13th century.

Dem 15. Jh. gehört die elegante Backsteinfassade des Rathauses zu *Hannover* an,
neben dem die Marktkirche (Mitte 14. Jh.) sichtbar wird.

The elegant 15th century brick façade of *Hanover* Townhall next to the Marktkirche (mid-14th century).

Die Zierwand des *Stralsunder* Rathauses (spätes 14. Jh.) vor dem mächtigen Turmpaar von St. Nikolai verkörpert Geist und Größe der hansischen Welt.

The ornamental wall of *Stralsund* Townhall (late 14th century)
standing before the mighty twin towers of St. Nikolai embodies the spirit and greatness of the Hanseatic world.

Nowak

In der Spätgotik findet baukünstlerische Ausdruckssprache Eingang in die Wehrarchitektur.
Links: Das Ünglinger Tor in *Stendal* (nach 1400). Oben: Der Hochmeisterpalast der *Marienburg* (um 1400).

Beauty and artistry were introduced into town-defences during the Late Gothic period.
Left: the Ünglinger Tor in *Stendal*, Germany (post 1400). Above: the High Master's Palace at *Marienburg* on the Nogat (c. 1400).

155

Trotz gotischer Formelemente verrät die Anfang des 14. Jh. errichtete Fassade des Domes von *Orvieto* bereits eine Renaissancegesinnung.

The early 14th century Gothic façade of *Orvieto* Cathedral already seems to herald the Renaissance.

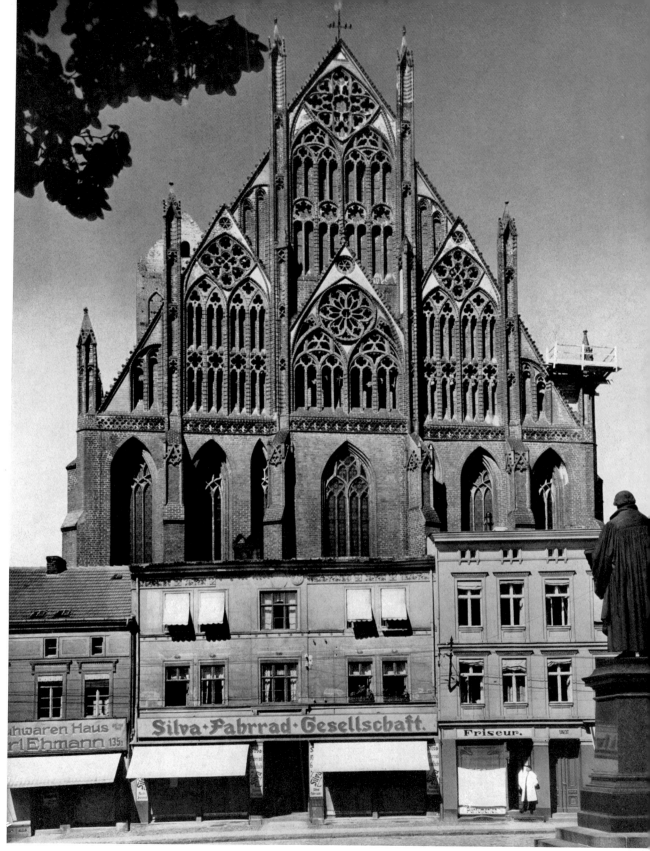

R. Müller

157 Die Spätgotik des Nordens hat manche Züge mit der Frührenaissance des Südens gemein. Chor der Marienkirche (um 1360) zu *Prenzlau*.
Northern Late Gothic and southern Renaissance style have some features in common. Choir of the Marienkirche (c. 1360) in *Prenzlau*.

Wie stark im 14. Jh. die Wandfläche und ruhiges Gleichmaß
wieder betont werden, zeigt ein Blick auf die Fassade der Heiligkreuzkirche in *Schwäbisch Gmünd*.

The façade of the Heiligkreuzkirche in *Schwäbisch Gmünd*,
an example of the stress laid by the 14th century on symmetry and wall-construction.

Aufsberg

Auch in der Disposition des Außengewändes trägt der spätgotische Chor (1445–1472) von St. Lorenz in *Nürnberg* Merkmale einer wohlabgewogenen Flächengliederung.

Traces of a new attitude to wall proportions are to be seen in the design of the Late Gothic choir at St. Lorenz', *Nuremberg* (1445–1472).

159

Blick in das Innere des St.-Veits-Doms von *Prag* (nach 1344), der, durch Matthias von Arras begonnen, von Peter Parler weitergebaut wurde.
View from the triforium of the interior of *Prague* Cathedral (post 1344), begun by Matthias of Arras who was followed by Peter Parler.

160

Der raumweite Hallenchor von St. Lorenz in *Nürnberg* ist um 1460 in bewußtem Gegensatz zur Enge von Langhaus und Seitenschiff angelegt worden.
The wide ''hall-choir'' of St. Lorenz', *Nuremberg*, was planned c. 1460 as a reaction against the narrow effect of nave and aisles.

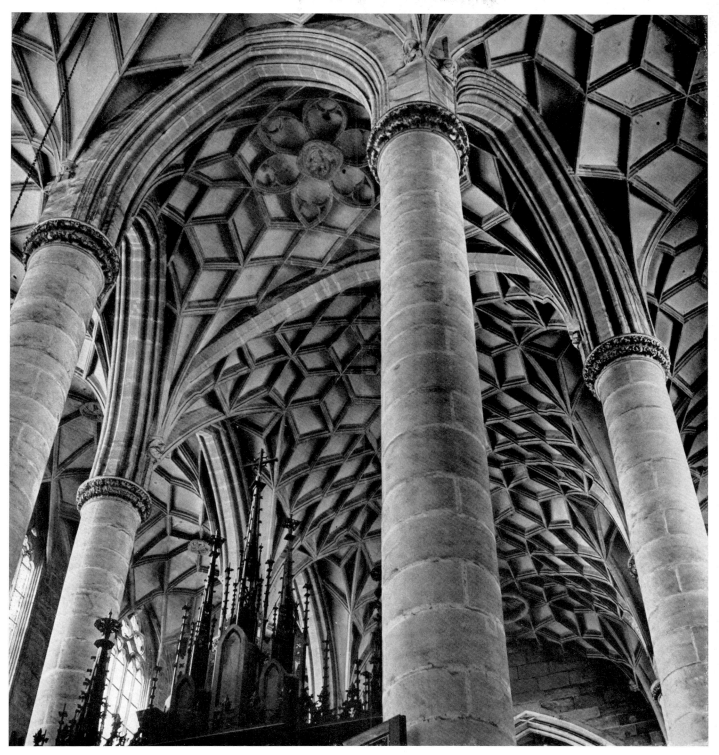

Jeiter

Immer reicher werden die Deckenkonstruktionen,
selbst in den ursprünglich schlichten Zisterzienserklöstern.
Das Gewölbe (um 1500) in der Klosterkirche *Maulbronn* (Ende 12. Jh.).

Even the ceilings of the originally plain Cistercian monasteries
grew more and more lavish in decoration.
The vault (c. 1500) of the conventual church at *Maulbronn* (late 12th c.).

Der Chor der Heiligkreuzkirche in *Schwäbisch Gmünd* (um 1350)
offenbart das neue, spätgotische Raumgefühl des Hallenbaus.
Blick in die Netzgewölbe.

The choir of the Heiligkreuzkirche in *Schwäbisch Gmünd* (c. 1350)
reveals the new Late Gothic feeling of space found in the "hall-church".
View of the net-vaulting.

Felton

Das Vorherrschen senkrechter Maßwerkstäbe wird in England „Perpendicular style" genannt.
Oben: Blick ins westliche Querhaus von *Canterbury*. Rechts: Westfassade der *Stralsunder* Marienkirche (nach 1382).

The predominance of vertical lines of tracery constitutes the English Perpendicular style.
Above: view of the Western Transept of *Canterbury*. Right: West Façade of the Marienkirche (post 1382) in *Stralsund*, Germany.

16

65

← Haustein

Gleich Mahnmalen
ragen die Türme
seenaher Städte
in Nordeuropa auf.
Links: Der Turm
der 1343–1502 errichteten
Marienkirche in *Danzig*.
Rechts: Der Turm von
t. Rombout in *Mecheln* (1341).

The towers of towns lying
along or near the
N. European coastline
have similar characteristics.
Left: the tower of the
Marienkirche, *Danzig*,
built between 1343 and 1502.
Right: the tower of
t. Rombout, *Malines* (1341).

Beispiele der Hochgotik in den Niederlanden. Links: Blick in den Chor der Anf. d. 14. Jh. entstandenen Grote Kerk zu *Brouwershaven* auf der Insel Schouwen-Duiveland. Oben: Die Oude Kerk im Herzen von *Amsterdam*, 1306 geweiht, aber bis ins 16. Jh. unaufhörlich umgebaut.

Examples of High Gothic in the Netherlands. Left: view of the early 14th century choir of the Grote Kerk at *Brouwershaven* on the isle of Schouwen-Duiveland. Above: the Oude Kerk in the heart of *Amsterdam*, consecrated in 1306 but under continuous construction until the 16th century.

Die Kathedrale von *Peterborough* in England (1201—1222).
Charakteristisch für England die Reihung gleicher Architekturelemente —
aber auch die eigenwillige Lösung, die mittlere
der hohen Portalöffnungen am schmalsten zu gestalten.

Peterborough Cathedral in England (1201—1222).
The West Front with its three immense portals
placed side by side, the narrowest in the centre,
has features which are typically English.

Immer wieder werden die Fluchten der ungewöhnlich lang gebaute
englischen Kathedralen von Querriegeln verstell
Das von der Tendenz der Vertikalen beherrschte Langhaus (nach 139
der Kathedrale von *Canterbury*

One sometimes finds that the naves and aisles of the exceptionall
long English cathedrals are dominated by cross-support
The nave (post 1390) of *Canterbury* Cathedr
where the emphasis is on the vertica

17

71

Ein eindringliches Bild vom vertikalen Maßwerk des Perpendikularstiles, das unvermittelt gegen die Kurve des Spitzbogens stößt: die Westfassade der Kathedrale in *Winchester* (nach 1350).

An impressive picture of Perpendicular style tracery in which the verticals start directly from the curve of the ogee. The West Front of *Winchester* Cathedral (post 1350).

Felton

Die Kathedrale von *Gloucester*, die Geburtsstätte des englischen Perpendikularstiles, birgt das Grab Eduards II. mit üppigem, spätgotischem Aufbau.

Gloucester Cathedral, birthplace of the Perpendicular Style, contains the Late Gothic, lavishly sculptured shrine of Edward II.

Anderson

Blick auf die mächtigen Pfeiler des *Mailänder* Domes,
inzigartig im Figurenschmuck der Kapitelle.

View of the huge piers of *Milan* Cathedral,
unique in the decoration of their capitals.

Der *Mailänder* Dom, mit dem man die nördliche Gotik zu übertreffen dachte, ist ein Werk
des Spätstils. Bezeichnend die starke Betonung des Details — der Dom zählt 135 Spitzen.

Milan Cathedral which it was hoped would surpass creations of northern Gothic art
is a work of the later style showing strong emphasis on detail. There are 135 miniature spires.

In *Venedigs* goldenem Zeitalter haben Giovanni und Bartolomeo Bon um 1430 den elegantesten Marmorpalast der Stadt, die Ca d'Oro, im Stil der Spätgotik geschaffen.

The Golden Age of *Venice* saw the creation (c. 1430) by Giovanni and Bartolomeo Bon of the most elegant marble palace in the city, the Ca d'Oro. It is in the Late Gothic style.

Der Dogenpalast in *Venedig*, höchster Ausdruck des Glanzes und Ruhmes der Seestadt, wurde 1309–1404 errichtet.
Unübersehbar sind die Anklänge an orientalische Architekturen.

The Doge's Palace in *Venice*, erected between 1309 and 1404, embodies all the glamour and renown of the maritime state.
It bears an unmistakable resemblance to oriental works of architecture.

Das 1402–1450 erbaute *Brüsseler* Rathaus, mehrfach restauriert,
atmet noch heute den Geist des stolzen Bürgertums spätgotischer Zeit.

Brussels Townhall, built between 1402 and 1450 and much restored,
still has something of the spirit of the proud citizens during the Late Gothic period.

Ein Spitzenwerk aus Stein, den großen Reliquienschreinen vergleichbar:
das Rathaus von *Loewen* in Belgien (1448–1463).

Stone-filigree work comparable to that of the great shrines:
Louvain Townhall in Belgium (1448–1463).

Wien, Stephansdom. Oben: Charakteristisch für das räumliche Empfinden der Spätgotik – das Relief im Tympanon des Singertores (1440–1450).
Rechts: Der mächtige, 1407–1433 errichtete Turm ist das Wahrzeichen der Stadt.

The Stephansdom in *Vienna*. Above: the relief on the tympanum of the Singertor (1440–1450) is typical of the Late Gothic feeling of space.
Right: the huge tower (1407–1433) is a town-landmark.

Seitenschiff
der St. Georgskirche
in *Dinkelsbühl* (1448–1492),
wohl der reifsten
spätgotischen Hallenkirche.

Aisle of St. George's
in *Dinkelsbühl* (1448–1492),
the most mature
of Late Gothic
"hall-churches".

Die Annenkirche (1499–1520)
im erzgebirgischen *Annaberg*
eine Hallenkirche mit der
reizvollen Spiel einand
durchflechtender Gewölberippen

The Annenkirche (1499–1520)
at *Annaberg*, Germany
a "hall-church" with
beautifully interlace
rib-vaulting

Kreuzgang der Kathedrale von *Gloucester*
mit 1351–1377 entstandenen Fächergewölben, den frühesten ihrer Art.

Cloisters of *Cloucester* Cathedral with their fan-vaulting (1351–1377),
the earliest of its kind.

Über die gesamte Raumbreite erstreckt sich das Fächergewölb[e]
der King's College Chapel (1446–1515) in *Cambridge*

The fan-vaulting of King's College Chapel (1446–1515) in *Cambridg[e]*
covers the breadth of the whole space

Umschau-Archiv

Die kurz nach 1500 geformten Sterngewölbe
der Marienkirche in *Danzig*.

The star-vaulting in the Marienkirche *(Danzig)*
dates from the early 16th century.

Zeugnis einer späten eigenständigen Entwicklung portugiesischer Gotik
die Konventskirche von *Belem*, deren Netzgewölbe 1500—1522 enstanden

The conventual church of *Belem* with its net-vaulting (1500—1522)
is a late independent development of Portuguese Gothic

Foto Marburg

Salamanca, Neue Kathedrale. Links: Das dreischiffige Innere (beg. 1513) mit Sterngewölben nach deutschem Vorbild.
Oben: Maurisch-orientalische Einflüsse verrät das im sog. Isabellastil errichtete mittlere Nordportal.

The New Cathedral at *Salamanca*. The three-aisled interior (1513 seqq.) boasts a star-vault on German lines.
Above: the centre North Portal built in the so-called "Isabella style" suggests Moorish-Oriental influences.

Der Flamboyantstil kam über England nach Frankreich. Oben: Rose (Anfang 16. Jh.) von Notre Dame in *Rouen*.
Rechts: Die Querschiffsfassade (16. Jh.) des mächtigen Kirchentorsos von St. Pierre in *Beauvais*.

The Flamboyant Style came to France via England. Above: rose-window (early 16th century) of Notre-Dame in *Rouen*.
Right: the 16th century Transept Façade of the huge and towerless church of St. Pierre in *Beauvais*.

192

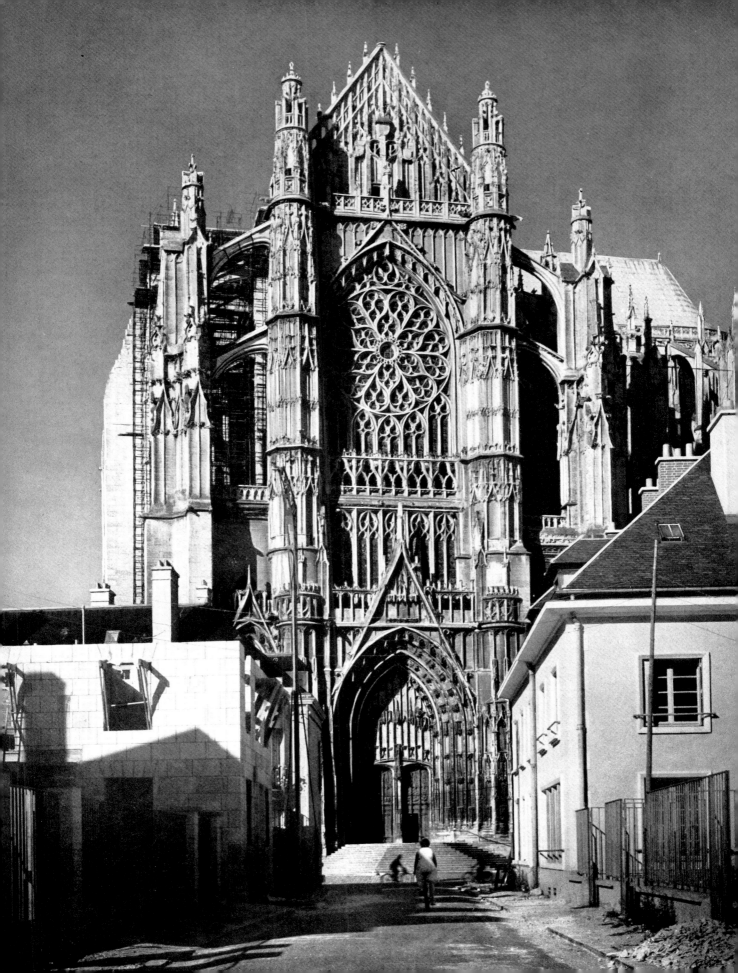

— Kersting

Die aufsteigende Tendenz der Gotik,
in ihr Gegenteil verkehrt:
Hängegewölbe in englischen
Bauwerken um 1500.
Links: Westminster Abbey, *London*.
Kapelle Heinrichs VII.
Rechts: Die unter Eduard IV.
begonnene St. Georgskapelle
in *Windsor Castle* — ein Schwanengesang
englischer Spätgotik.

The upward surge of Gothic inverted:
hanging vaults in English buildings
dating from c. 1500.
Left: Henry VII's Chapel
at Westminster Abbey, *London*.
Right: St. George's Chapel at *Windsor*,
a swansong of English Late Gothic.

Felton

Stone

Die Kathedrale von *Canterbury* gilt als ein Spiegel englischer Architekturgeschichte vom 13. bis 15. Jh.
Das Gewölbe des Kreuzgangs mit der aus Wappensteinen gebildeten Kielleiste.

Canterbury Cathedral is considered to be a reflection of English architectural history of the 13th — 15th centuries.
The vaulting of the cloisters with the ridge-rib formed of stone coats-of-arms.

Eines der im Grunde schon renaissancehaften Raumgebilde der Spätgotik,
die Divinity School in *Oxford*, erbaut von Thomas Elkyn.

The Late Gothic Divinity School at *Oxford*, built by Thomas Elkyn
really already shows the Renaissance attitude to space.

197

← Jeiter →

Kloster *Batalha*. Maßlos ist die Prachtentfaltung portugiesischer Spätgotik, zu deren Ornamentik die Kunst vieler Länder als Vorbild gedient hat. Brunnenkapelle (rechts) und Maßwerkfenster des Kreuzgangs (oben, beg. 1387, ausgebaut 15. Jh.).

The magnificence of Portuguese Late Gothic knows no bounds. Ideas on ornamentation were borrowed from many countries. *Batalha* Monastery, "Fountain Chapel" (right) and window-tracery of the cloisters (above, begun in 1387, completed 15th ct.).

Felton

an den Kathedralen gebaut. Die Kathedrale in *Oxford,* die kleinste in England, durchmißt von den Fundamenten

alle Entwicklungsepochen der Architektur von der normannischen Romanik bis zum Ausklang der Gotik.

the result of centuries of labour. *Oxford* Cathedral, the smallest in England,

on to vaults all architectural developments from Norman to Late Gothic.